IDENTITY
REVEALED

A DEVOTIONAL STUDY IN COLOSSIANS

AMY REARDON

wesleyan
PUBLISHING HOUSE
wphstore.com
Indianapolis, Indiana

CREST BOOKS

CONTENTS

Dedicated to my husband, Rob,
for his constant support and encouragement,
and to my dear friends, Karen and Nuvi Mehta,
for providing time and space for this project.

INTRODUCTION

It is hard to imagine what a shock to the first-century world Christianity must have been. Was it a new religion or was it a sect of Judaism? Even its strongest proponents seemed unclear on that. The movement revolved around a humble man who had walked the earth, whom many had seen and physically touched. While it claimed to change people internally, Christianity was also outwardly focused: it involved forgiveness, grace, and care for the helpless. And this new approach to faith—this gospel—not only accepted people from different nations, but it also actively *sought* them. It intentionally broke down barriers. It was strange. It was different. But it was beautiful and attracted people in throngs.

Even the people of the church in Colossae had much to figure out. They had just adopted an entire new belief system, a new Lord, a new life. In order to help them navigate all this, the apostle Paul wrote them a letter that spoke a great deal about identity: who Christ was and who they were as believers in Christ.

It is well accepted that Paul wrote the book of Colossians. Scholars with theories contrary to historical claims pop up from time to time, but objections to acknowledging Paul as author are minimal. The exact circumstances in which he wrote, however, are a bit more debated, as we will explore in the following section.

THE AUTHOR'S ENVIRONS

The date Paul wrote Colossians has not been positively proven, but the book was likely written around the year AD 60. Paul was in prison; this is made clear by his reference to being "in chains" in 4:3 and to "fellow prisoner" Aristarchus in 4:10. The book of Acts describes how Paul was imprisoned three times: overnight, in Philippi (see Acts 16:23–40); for two years, in Caesarea (see Acts 24:27); and in his rented home in Rome—an imprisonment that lasted two years but came with some privileges (see Acts 28:30–31).

Here's where the question arises: while most experts agree that Paul wrote during his Roman imprisonment, the theory does pose a few problems. For example, Paul would not have been "in chains" while on house arrest in Rome (though he could have been speaking figuratively). Also, trips made by Onesimus and Epaphras from Paul's location to Colossae are mentioned rather casually. Rome was about 1,200 miles from Colossae—no small trip in the first century, or even today!

Many Bible scholars find it highly probable that Paul spent time in prison in Ephesus, though it isn't mentioned in Acts or explicitly in any of the epistles. N. T. Wright suggests that imprisonment there can be "inferred from 2 Cor. 1:8, 1 Cor. 15:32."[1] Therefore, the strong possibility exists that Paul was in Ephesus when he wrote Colossians. It was only one hundred miles from Colossae, which would have made travel more reasonable for Paul's messengers, and some suggest that the list of people who were with Paul (see Col. 4:10–14) were more likely to be found in Ephesus than Rome.

Does Paul's location have any bearing on how we read and understand this epistle? Not really. But we can draw inspiration concerning our own service for God when we consider Paul's circumstances. The fact that he wrote and ministered and prayed fervently for others while in prison can and should encourage us to approach the tasks God has for us with bravery and tenacity. Even being imprisoned in one's own home, as Paul was in Rome, could easily sour a person toward his gospel mission. But Paul became neither bitter nor self-reflective; his concern was always for new believers and his ministry was styled for maximum benefit. Whether Paul was in chains in Ephesus, housebound in Rome, or in some other confined circumstance, he rejoiced in his predicament for the sake of the church (see 1:24).

THE RECIPIENTS

Colossae was a once-important city that was in decline. Sitting on the banks of the Lycus River, Colossae had previously risen to prominence through its wool industry. The region, which included the city of Laodicea, suffered frequent earthquakes, including a significant one around the time that the book of Colossians was written. Laodicea recovered from that earthquake, but the same money and effort were not invested into Colossae because it was already waning economically.

The Lycus Valley had plenty of Jewish influence, but Paul's repeated reference to his readers' pagan past implies that the majority of the Colossians Christians were Gentile converts.

Paul had evangelized this region of the world—Asia Minor—but had not gone to Colossae. There was a large

Jewish influence in and around Colossae, but most of the people in the area had been raised with pagan beliefs.

We conclude from Paul's comments early in chapter 1 that the Colossians had learned the gospel from Epaphras, who was from that city himself, and whom Paul referred to in 1:7 as his "fellow servant." Although F. F. Bruce, a prominent New Testament scholar, claimed that Colossae was still a major city during Paul's day, perhaps the fact that Paul did not make a trip there validates the more popular theory that Colossae was no longer the vital city it had once been.[2]

Regardless, the gospel had taken root there—and Paul took notice. While Colossae may have been a dying city in some ways, some of its citizens had received new life in Christ!

THE REASON

The overwhelming majority of scholars believe that heretical teaching was sweeping through the Colossian church.[3] Paul's first purpose for writing would have been to reestablish Christ—no one else, and no other religious practice—as the means of salvation.

Several passages in Colossians seem to poke holes in particular heresies that were common among early Christians.

A number of false teachings have been proposed as the problem in Colossae, but I would suggest that Paul addressed more than one of them. Let us entertain the possibility that several of these bad ideas were threatening the doctrine of the Colossian church:

- **Judaism, adopted by Gentiles:** New converts who lived in the pagan world wondered whether they must fulfill the Jewish law to be true Christians, since Christianity came out of Judaism. N. T. Wright notes, "It is this tendency that Paul is resolutely opposing in, for instance, Galatians, and in Philippians 3. It is my contention that a similar danger was the reason for the writing of Colossians, at least chapter 2."[4]

- **Jewish mysticism:** F. F. Bruce observed, "While the Colossian heresy was basically Jewish, it is not the straightforward Judaizing legalism of Galatians that is envisaged in Colossians, but a form of mysticism which tempted its adepts to look on themselves as a spiritual elite."[5] An example of those who saw themselves as "spiritual elite" were the Essenes, who thought they possessed certain mysteries of God that others could not access.

- **Syncretism:** Arthur Patzia points out that there seemed to exist a melding together of several ideas, including:

○ *Astrology*: "One of the basic tenets of astrology is that there is a correspondence between the movements of the gods above and the alterations that take place on earth."[6] This ideology may include worship of angels, a practice which is denounced in Colossians 2:18.

○ *Gnosticism*: There were various forms of gnosticism, but in all its forms, knowledge (*gnosis*)—usually secret knowledge revealed to spiritual elites—was prized and sought. A characteristic belief was dualism between spirit and matter, which included separation from God by several cosmic spheres, each one having its own rulers. Some gnostics had behavioral restrictions so their fleshly nature didn't control them, which seem to be alluded to in Colossians 2:16 and 23. Other gnostics were licentious, caving in to the evils of the flesh but separating that from the purity of the spirit.[7]

○ *Mystery religions*: This general category includes a variety of belief systems that had secret teaching and rituals. As with Jewish mysticism and Gnosticism, those who were on the inside were thought to be on a different plane than others, possessing exceptional knowledge of the mysteries of the universe. This kind of thinking caused divisions among people, separating the enlightened from the prosaic.

○ *Hellenistic Judaism*: According to Patzia, "This is not . . . the orthodox Judaism of Palestine; rather, it is a Judaism that has been thoroughly Hellenized [given a Greek adaptation]." Jewish practices are referred to (2:11, 16, 18) and the people of Colossae were concerned that they might be compelled to follow Jewish practices despite the freedom Christ promised.[8]

While establishing what Christianity *is not*, Paul also established for his readers what it *is*. The book of Colossians explained to believers what it is to find their identities in Christ: the freedom from Hebrew regulation that Christ provides, the contrast between their prior nature and their reborn selves, and how Christ provided salvation and strength for them. It taught the Colossians how to shed their previous lifestyle and embrace what Christ had created and was creating them to be.

Much of the book of Colossians was written as a defense of critical principles. This defense was not something negative; it was intended to build truth and understanding. Colossians was written in a loving tone. The whole of it was nurturing—Paul's tone was almost fatherly. The most helpful thing that could be done for the people of Colossae was to dismantle their misunderstandings gently.

Straight out of the gate, Paul began with a defense of the glory and supremacy of Christ. He moved on to defend the truth of the gospel against heresy in a variety of ways. Finally, he defended full liberty in Christ: liberty from rules and rituals that no longer had bearing on a person's standing before God; liberty from society's mores in favor of God's priorities; liberty from the old, sinful self, who is replaced with the new Christ-ruled self. The new identity of Christ's people is that of a liberated humanity.

Many people today—even followers of Jesus—struggle to define exactly what Christianity is. Just like in Colossae, the world today is fraught with misunderstanding, confusion, and deception. And so, Colossians still speaks. Let us explore what it has to say to us.

1

FROM APOSTLE TO SAINTS

COLOSSIANS 1:1–2

On January 21, 2019, it was announced that Edgar Martinez, a native Puerto Rican who had spent his entire baseball career as a Seattle Mariner, would be inducted into the Baseball Hall of Fame. The next day, the *Seattle Times* featured a story about Martinez. His brother told the reporter that when they were children he would pitch rocks to Edgar for hours and he would bat them with a broom handle.[1] Martinez's story is one of metamorphosis: from an impoverished little boy who didn't even own a bat and ball, to a wealthy, famous major league baseball star honored as one of the best in his profession. We may not think our lives are as exceptional as Edgar Martinez's— but really they are! We have been and are being transformed and we claim a different identity from who we once were. Once we were spiritually impoverished and ill-equipped for living a godly life. Now we have access to everything we need.

APOSTLE, BY GOD'S WILL (COL. 1:1)

The book of Colossians begins with Paul establishing his authority, granted to him by God as a result of the transformation Christ had brought about in his life. Unlike the Corinthian and Galatian churches, the church at Colossae had not actually challenged Paul's authority. Nevertheless, it was fitting for him to establish himself before giving instruction from the Lord to them. So he identified himself as an apostle, chosen by God's will.

While it is sometimes suggested that an apostle had to receive a commission directly from Christ, the use of the word *apostle* is not so stringent in every case throughout the New Testament (see Acts 1:26, 14:14; Rom. 16:7). One could effectively argue that an apostle was a person whose entire life was committed to spreading the gospel and further educating those who already embraced it. Paul qualified on both counts. He was chosen and commissioned by Christ on the road to Damascus (see Acts 9), and he gave his life over to the mission of spreading the good news of Christ. For the sake of the gospel he had:

Been in prison more frequently, been flogged more severely, and been exposed to death again and again. Five times I received from the Jews the forty lashes minus one. Three times I was beaten with rods, once I was pelted with stones, three times I was shipwrecked, I spent a night and a day in the open sea, I have been constantly on the move. I have been in danger from rivers, in danger from bandits, in danger from my fellow Jews, in danger from Gentiles; in danger in the city, in danger in the country, in danger at sea; and in danger from false believers. I have labored and toiled and have often gone without sleep; I have known hunger and thirst and have often gone without food; I have been cold and naked. Besides everything else, I face daily the pressure of my concern for all the churches. (2 Cor. 11:23–28)

Paul wanted the Colossians to remember that his role as an apostle was by the will of God. It is doubtful that anyone could be an apostle outside the will of God, so why did Paul stress this? He wanted to remind his readers that the calling on his life could not have been misinterpreted. It was direct and specific: he encountered Christ while traveling to persecute Christians. There were witnesses:

The men traveling with Saul [later referred to as "Paul"] stood there speechless; they heard the sound but did not see anyone. (Acts 9:7)

But the Lord said to Ananias, "Go! This man [Saul/Paul] is my chosen instrument to proclaim my name to the Gentiles and their kings and to the people of Israel." (Acts 9:15)

Paul stressed that his mission was through the will of God so that the important things he needed to say would be accepted readily.

God calls all believers to share the gospel, and sometimes he gives very specific direction to people of his choosing. Occasionally—regrettably—some people claim to be appointed or called to something God has never asked them to do. In the church, we must be careful to know the difference. I once saw a woman usurp a beautiful Sunday morning worship service with an unnecessary admonition to the congregation, claiming she had a "word from the Lord," while in fact all she did was summarize the poignant sermon we had just heard. People absolutely get timely, particular messages from God, but we must be discerning as to what is really of God and what isn't.

In the case of Paul, his vision of Christ, heard by those who were with him and attested to by God Himself to Christians in Damascus, was an obvious stamp of authority on his life. One of the strongest ways that we can affirm that something is the will of God is by checking with other believers in our Christian community to see whether they are convinced of the same.

GOD'S HOLY PEOPLE (COL. 1:2)

Names and titles are important in the Bible. Abram became Abraham. Jacob became Israel. Gideon was given the title of "mighty warrior." Saul became Paul. The names represented a permanent change in those men. Names and titles are important in society today. We identify ourselves by titles: I'm a mother, a wife, a Salvation Army officer, a Seahawks fan, and so on. The more I own these titles, the more I live up to them. I could also tell you that I'm a Libra—but I don't care about that one iota; I don't own it so it doesn't impact the way I view myself.

Many Christians refer to themselves as "a sinner saved by grace." This phrase is interesting. It is helpful in that it reminds us of our imperfection and the ease with which we could revert to our old ways. But as a nameplate metaphorically worn on the foreheads of God's children, it doesn't seem very theologically sound.

As we will see as we progress through the book, Colossians teaches us about our identity in Christ. To identify ourselves as sinners is to identify with who we *were*. Isn't it more helpful to identify ourselves as who we *are* and who we *are becoming* in Christ? Shouldn't we wear the title that God has given to us as a result of the liberating work of Jesus Christ, rather than the title that hearkens back to our days of slavery? I do not say that Christians will not sin. But I do say that we have been given a new name, and it is *saint*, not *sinner*. When we sin, it is a slipup; it is not the normal order of things. It is not what defines us. If we are to grasp our identity in Christ, we must understand holiness (not carnality) to be our skeletal structure.

The people of Colossae were holy people: saints.[2] They were the faithful brothers and sisters in Christ. To address them in this way was to honor what Christ had done in their lives. Our impression of their faithfulness to God wouldn't be the same if Paul had written: "To the sinners saved by grace in Colossae."

GRACE AND PEACE (COL. 1:2)

"Grace and peace" is a typical greeting or benediction in the letters of the New Testament. It bestows blessing and approval. Even today, many Christians use these words or something similar as a sign-off on an email or other communication.

Of course, one person can't pass God's grace on to another. *Grace*, as Paul defined it, is strictly the work of God, between God and an individual. In Romans 3:24 he wrote: "All are justified freely by his grace through the redemption that came by Christ Jesus." By speaking grace from the Father upon his readers at the onset of the book of Colossians, Paul expressed his great hope that his readers would experience a deeper understanding of the grace God had already given them.

Paul also wished peace upon the people. Though the book was written in Greek, the word *eirene* that Paul used reflects on the Jewish idea of *shalom*. Shalom is not always readily understood by English speakers. We translate the word as *peace*, but it means more than the absence of war, the absence of fighting, and the presence of calmness. Shalom is peace in every aspect of a human life: it is spiritual and physical wholeness and wellness.

We can't control many circumstances in our lives. Shalom doesn't mean that our house is clean and our kids are behaving and the mortgage has been paid off. But shalom occurs when we are spiritually and emotionally whole and unrattled in the midst of the burdens and surprises of life.

REFLECTION QUESTIONS

1. Paul established himself as an apostle, and his life proved his worthiness to speak on the Lord's behalf. What kind of barometer do you use to judge whether a person has enough spiritual authority to speak into your life?

2. Have you ever received what you considered to be a specific message from God? How did it come to you and how did you verify it?

3. I've expressed my feeling about the common phrase "a sinner saved by grace." What are *your* thoughts on it?

4. What do you think it means to be a *saint*, as Paul used the term?

5. Do you know someone (or are you someone) who demonstrates a shalom-style peace even during hardship? What does that look like?

2

THE PEOPLE OF GOD

COLOSSIANS 1:3–8

When I met Loreen, she was a college student whose intelligence outstripped her emotional capacity. It was easy to see that she was brimming with potential, but she seemed rather lost and looking for someone to latch onto. Someone who would offer her a listening ear. Someone who would offer her grace. I realized that the Lord was calling me to invest in her—to give her my time, my attention, my heart—though I barely knew her. Over a decade later, this girl, who started out as something of a "project" of mine, has become one of the most important people in my life. The relationship is deeper and fuller than I ever anticipated, and means as much to me as it does to her.

The verses we will look at in this study are about investing in others, even when they aren't people of our own circle.

UNEXPECTED UNITY (COL. 1:3–4)

We can find both unity and approval in these simple verses. Paul used the word *we* instead of *I* because he and Timothy were of like mind in their appreciation for the Colossians, and they joined together to pray for them. Their brotherly bond extended to the Colossians, because the Holy Spirit links as siblings those for whom we pray. In every other way, these people were strangers; Paul did not know the Colossians. But through the Holy Spirit they were profoundly connected. Paul and Timothy, then, found joy in people they'd never met, prayed for them, and had enough concern to write an epistle to them.

Let us not miss the dramatic element here. Prior to his Damascus-road experience, Paul (Saul) would not have given these people the time of day. Now he wrote with endorsement and complete acceptance. Surely the Colossians, too, would have been coolly indifferent to people such as Paul and Timothy prior to their own conversions. Now they were acclaimed for their "love . . . for all God's people."

As we are joined to the body of Christ, natural divisions become unnatural. The image of the body, which Paul used in other letters (see 1 Cor. 12:12–27; Rom. 12:4-5; Eph. 3:6), underscores this newfound unity. This metaphor is critical to our new identity in Christ. We all belong to each other. "For we were all baptized by one Spirit so as to form one body—whether Jews or Gentiles, slave or free," Paul wrote in 1 Corinthians 12:13. How can the foot be unconcerned with the eye, even though they may look nothing alike and function in different ways?

Have you ever had a toothache that made you feel miserable all over? Though it seems as if it should be an isolated annoyance, it somehow takes over the whole of your being. The body image Paul has given to us is effective because we relate very personally to the connectivity of the physical body. Though the body isn't referenced in Colossians 1, we are witnessing something powerful: the mysterious union of the dissimilar and foreign through the Holy Spirit because of the headship of Christ.

We must note something else in these verses. In other letters, Paul wished grace and peace from God the Father *and* the Lord Jesus Christ. Here, as he prepared to establish the authority of Christ and the relationship between the Father and the Son, he referred to "the Father *of* our Lord Jesus Christ" (emphasis mine). Christ is something other than earthly Messiah; He is in father/son relationship with God in a way that none of the rest of us are. This change in preposition is a hint of the exposition to come regarding the nature of Jesus Christ and His relationship to the Father.

CORE COMPONENTS (COL. 1:5)

Three words in this verse are often found together in Paul's writings: faith, love, and hope. These words have no special connection that makes them appear together repeatedly other than that they are all core components of the belief system we embrace. Faith activates our salvation (see Rom. 3:25). Love is the most important thing of all, as Christ taught us (see Matt. 22:37–39). Hope is what drives our faith forward. Without hope in Christ's resurrection and what it means for our eternal future, "our preaching is useless and so is your faith," Paul said (1 Cor. 15:14). Our hope is not murky. We wait for the promised return of our King and the complete establishment of His kingdom. We wait for victory and eternal life. "If only for this life we have hope in Christ, we are of all people most to be pitied"—but, praise God—"in Christ all will be made alive." (1 Cor. 15:19, 22).

I knew a man of the Sikh faith whose life ended early. His family *hoped* that he had prayed and honored God enough that he would be reincarnated as something good and would be closer to reaching the ultimate goal of being one with God. But they couldn't be certain. He might have many more lives to live before his spirit could reach its ultimate goal. How different that is from what we believe as Christians! When we use the word *hope*, we really mean *certainty*. We are *certain* that the blood of Christ has cleared us of all debt before God and secured our position as children in His family. We are *certain* we will live eternally with Him.

When the pagans of Colossae heard the gospel, the idea of an eternal hope would have been a new concept for them. Because Paul said that faith and love spring from hope, we might guess that the Colossians latched onto the hope of eternal life first. That hope was what drew them to Christianity. Once drawn in, they attained faith and love, which they exercised regularly.

CREDIT WHERE IT IS DUE (COL. 1:6–8)

While Paul thanked the Colossians for their faithfulness and love, he gave credit where it was really due. It was the gospel itself that was bearing fruit and spurring growth. The credit did not belong to individuals—not even to Paul himself. Rather than applauding himself for spreading the news of Christ through the known world, he focused on the impact. Paul was only the messenger. He could not reform lives.

The first appointment that my husband and I had as Salvation Army corps officers (pastors) was in South Phoenix. I often cringe when I remember that appointment. My husband was his typical brilliant self, but my mistakes grossly outweighed my successes. I unwittingly offended people as I tried to establish my authority.

On top of that, we served a largely Hispanic population and I—not a Hispanic woman—made cultural blunders. I felt out of place and ineffective. But years later I encountered a young woman who had been a teenager when we were in Phoenix. She told me that I had been a role model for her and that she was preparing to go into full-time ministry. I had no idea I had made any impression on her at all. The truth was that despite my shortcomings, the gospel had gone forward. The Word of the Lord is quick and powerful and sharp. It easily overcame my failings and penetrated her heart.

It is comforting to know that the gospel does not rely upon our expertise in sharing it. It does, however, require our willingness.

Here Paul mentioned Epaphras. He was a faithful witness to the gospel, which changed the lives of many people in his city. But Epaphras was a religious outsider. The events that shaped the gospel—the life, death, and resurrection of Christ—took place in Israel, far from his home. So it stands to reason that Epaphras might have made a few theological mistakes or muddled a few historical details when sharing the gospel. He was not daunted, however. And because the gospel didn't depend upon human power, it flourished.

REFLECTION QUESTIONS

1. The gospel initiates unlikely friendships, as demonstrated by the affection Paul felt for the Colossians, whom he had never even met. People who would likely never be concerned about one another became bonded through Christ. Has this ever happened in your life?

2. Are there any groups of people that you would prefer to keep out of your life, rather than embrace them as brothers and sisters in Christ? If so, are you prepared to imitate the converted Jews and Gentiles of old and learn to include those you would rather ignore?

3. Hope seems to be what drew the Colossians to the gospel. What do you think draws people to the gospel today? How can we be sure to capitalize on that as we work to bring others into the kingdom?

4. Though several people are mentioned in Colossians 1:3–8, the emphasis is on God and the power of His gospel. List ways in which you see God being glorified in this small passage.

3

PAUL'S DESIRE FOR THE COLOSSIANS

COLOSSIANS 1:9–14

My husband and I have spent a good portion of our ministry working with young adults. I have concluded that the decade from ages twenty to thirty can be one of the most difficult times of life. Many earnest young people have approached us in angst over career choices, marriage, graduate school, having a baby, etc., wanting to be in accordance with God's will. We have constantly worked to persuade these young people that God's will has more to do with your daily behavior than which city you choose to live in. It's not that God does not care about the details of our lives, but His consistent will is that wherever we go, we live in the way He has instructed us.

Paul described the will of God in these verses. He often wrote long, complex sentences, as evidenced in the sentence that starts in the middle of verse 9 and stretches through verse 12. The bulk of this sentence can be broken down into phrases that answer the questions *what*, *how,* and *why*.

What did Paul desire for the Colossians?

• That they would be filled with the knowledge of God's will (v. 9)

How is God's will known?

• Through the wisdom and understanding that the Spirit gives (v. 9)

What kind of life is worthy of the Lord and pleases Him in every way?

• Bears good fruit (v. 10)
• Grows in the knowledge of God (v. 10)
• Endures in the faith (v. 11)
• Is patient (v. 11)
• Is joyfully thankful (v. 12)

How does a person become patient and enduring?

• Strength is given through God in His glorious might (v. 11)

KNOWLEDGE, WISDOM, AND UNDERSTANDING (COL. 1:9)

Throughout the book of Colossians Paul addressed heresy.[1] In verses 9–14 he began to counter heretical teaching, though the argument was subtle. The teachings of Gnosticism had almost certainly reached the ears of the Colossians. Gnostics believed that there was a higher, better spiritual knowledge that most people could not access. If such knowledge was revealed to you, then you were part of a spiritual elite. Paul dispensed with that idea by praying that God would fill the Colossians with knowledge of His will, wisdom, and understanding. The people would have taken note that this prayer was for *all* of them, not only a select few.

Nineteenth-century author George MacDonald wrote a beautiful novel called *Sir Gibbie* (written in 1879, but republished later under the title *The Baronet's Song*). The protagonist is a raggedy, homeless orphan named Gibbie who can't even speak. But his heart yearns for God and he lives in a way that is utterly holy. His goodness shines in contrast to the character of the clergyman of the town. This simple boy has the wisdom and understanding to live according to God's will, even though he is unable to articulate anything about it.

God's will is that people live holy lives, full of love for one another and full of love for God, and the knowledge to do so is given by the Holy Spirit to *all* who seek it. The *Life Application Bible Commentary* says: "This knowledge of God's will comes from wisdom and understanding. These are not merely abstract concepts; instead, Paul was referring to the true wisdom and understanding made available by God's Holy Spirit."[2]

BEARING FRUIT AND GROWING IN KNOWLEDGE (COL. 1:10)

The point of knowing God's will is to follow it, for when we do, our lives please God and are found worthy in His sight. Such a person bears fruit in all manner of good works and labors to increase her knowledge of God. If we were to make a list of all the "good works" in which a Christian could engage, we would probably never reach a point of conclusion. The idea is not that each of us must participate in every good work there is! Rather, whatever we undertake should be good in God's eyes and fruitful.

As I write, I am sitting in the living room of one of my closest friends. She and her husband have provided a writing retreat for me in their home. They are conducting a good work by allowing me this opportunity. Of course, my friend could have *attempted* a good work by suggesting the idea (which she did). But she *bore fruit* in this good work by going to great lengths to make sure I got here, I had quiet space, I was comfortable, and so on. She and her husband have done this to serve the Lord because they believe that the work I am doing is for His kingdom. Sometimes the good works that God asks us to do are creative and unexpected. It isn't always teaching Sunday school or volunteering at the food bank—though I certainly don't disparage those worthy deeds!

No doubt God is pleased whenever a person commits a selfless act. But our lives are deemed worthy when our works are motivated by our knowledge of God and done alongside our pursuit of Him. This pursuit involves personal and corporate study of Him. He has seen fit to gift us the written Word, which reveals much of who He is. God has also given us fellow believers, so that through writing or conversation we might learn more about God from each other.

It is fair to assume that you have opened this book with intent to increase your knowledge of God. I am a fellow Christian seeking to share the results of my study. If you and I were to sit together and you were to share your testimony or your interpretation of something you read in the Word today, my knowledge of God would be increased as well. We please God whenever we seek to know Him better, during times of formal Bible study as well as when discussing the goodness of God over coffee with a friend.

Coffee with a friend is not a substitute for daily Bible study. But it is unhealthy when a Christian only seeks to know God alone, with no input from the body of Christ. We should explore every means of learning God better! The greatest honor of our human lives is the ability to know our divine Lord.

ENDURANCE AND PATIENCE (COL. 1:11)

The standard for living a worthy life is high. To be fruitful in good works and pursue knowledge of God requires strength beyond what a human can consistently muster. Most people are just trying to be basically decent human beings. But God calls His people to more than that. His power alone is enough to provide the strength and endurance needed.

You can apply the principle of strength and endurance to everyday things, such as not losing your cool with your kids or not giving up on a project at work when things get tough. There is value in interpreting these verses that way. As we continue to read Colossians, however, we will see that something larger was at stake when Paul wrote the letter. He had to admonish the Colossians not to cave in to the false teachings that were assaulting their congregation, nor to turn away from Christ should they happen to face trials and persecution, as so many early Christians did.

Today, these verses teach us to access God's strength at all times, preparing us for the greatest trials of life as well as the smaller ones. Satan has not ceased his efforts to draw God's people away toward errant belief systems. Just as human philosophies tugged at the Colossians (see 2:8), we encounter many other approaches to life, and they have their allure. While some of us may be drawn to other religions, maybe even more of us are tempted by materialism, pleasure, or personal gain. There are also types of "Christian" belief systems that can nudge out the truth of Christian faith if we are not careful.

Remaining true to Christian doctrine is not our only show of endurance. God desires our lives to be characterized by patience at all levels. Having a firm grasp of Christian doctrine is not enough if we cannot demonstrate patience in ordinary situations and to the people around us.

JOYFUL THANKSGIVING (COL. 1:12)

Joy during struggle was one of Paul's consistent themes (see 2 Cor. 7:4; 1 Thess. 1:6). So it isn't surprising that when he wrote about patience and endurance to the Colossians, he turned to the subject of joy. The NIV says that we should endure *and* give thanks, but the NRSV translation says that we are to endure *while* giving thanks. The second has a stronger implication. Paul's exhortation to be joyful leaves no room for self-pity, even in the most difficult of circumstances. He certainly modeled that joy despite harrowing events in his life, which included imprisonments, shipwrecks, and even personal clashes with other Christian leaders.

The discipline of walking barefoot on top of burning coals is practiced in many cultures, but the purpose may not seem clear to some of us. It seems to be a demonstration of man mastering the elements, stoically bearing up to any challenge even when danger is present. One might be tempted to view Christian joy in the same way, as if our joy is contradictory to our predicament—just a show of stoicism with a somewhat nebulous purpose. But it's not that way at all. Our joy, though it may be challenging at times, is utterly justified. It is predicated on the fact that we are part of the inheritance of God in the kingdom of light.

INTO THE LIGHT (COL. 1:12–14)

In study 2, we took a look at how the wall between Christian Jews and Gentiles was being dismantled. Further evidence is seen here, as Paul noted that the Father qualified the Colossians to share in the inheritance of the "holy people" or "saints" (meaning member of the church, in this context). F. F. Bruce writes: "[T]hese Colossian Christians are no longer 'strangers and sojourners,' although they were Gentiles by birth; they have been reborn into the family of God, thanks to their all-enabling Father."[3]

Religions were very regionally specific in those days, and the Jewish people often demonstrated a smug attitude toward Gentiles. But Paul made it clear that these particular Gentiles were as much a part of the inheritance as any other "holy person" or "saint."

In the Old Testament the inheritance of the Jews had been the Promised Land. For those belonging to Christ, the inheritance is far broader. The *Life Application Commentary* notes, "God's people in the New Testament are the very sons of God, and as such they have the right to inherit Christ and a glorious eternity in the light. The promise of land is broadened to include the whole creation."[4]

This "kingdom of light" is also called the "kingdom of the Son" in the next verse. It is in contrast to the "dominion of darkness" from which we were rescued. Paul's testimony, the Colossians' testimony, my testimony, and your testimony are summed up in verses 13 and 14: our rescue, our inclusion, our redemption (freedom), and our forgiveness. All these are further reasons to rejoice!

Though we are so unworthy on our own, God qualified us, through the sacrifice of Jesus, to be part of His family of heirs. He grabbed us from the dungeon of the enemy and brought us to the palace of His love. We were not fit to be there. We were ratty, dirty, unrefined. But He cleansed us by forgiving our sins, and He continues to refine us. We belong now.

REFLECTION QUESTIONS

1. According to this passage, how are we to know God's will?

2. List the things in this passage that are said to be worthy and to please the Lord. How are those attributes being played out in your life? In what ways could you improve?

3. Is there another faith system, philosophy, or lifestyle that sometimes tempts you to set aside your Christian faith? How can you call on God's strength?

4. When or in what way did the Lord rescue you from the dominion of darkness and bring you into the kingdom of the Son He loves?

4

THE SUPREMACY OF CHRIST

COLOSSIANS 1:15–20

When I was young we used to sing a chorus in church that said, "Christ is all, yes, all in all. My Christ is all in all." I interpreted that song as a personal proclamation that I had put Christ first in my life. He was all *to me*. But that simple chorus comes to mind when I read the lofty words of the ancient hymn that is Colossians 1:15–20. In this stirring passage Christ is portrayed as Creator, as the supreme and eternal One, and as the Redeemer of all that has fallen away from Him. What He created, He reigns over, and what He created, He saves. He is all in all.

One of the things that makes this passage stunning is that it moves from His supremacy to His sacrifice, from acme to nadir—pinnacle to rock bottom, within the space of one paragraph. After extolling Christ as Maker and Master of the Universe, Paul reminded us that He stooped so low as to die a humiliating death for the sake of our reconciliation.

LITERARY TECHNIQUES (COL. 1:15–20)

Depending on which version of the Bible you use, these verses may be printed as a poem or hymn. Many scholars think that these words were not Paul's, but that he inserted a commonly sung hymn.[1] Hymns of that day were rhythmic and singable, but they were also creed-like, delineating the fundamentals of the faith (as are many hymns today). The hymn can be split into three strophes with different emphases:

- Verses 15–16: Christ the Creator
- Verses 17–18: Christ the Lord of All
- Verses 19–20: Christ the Reconciler

Another structural element that has poetic beauty and theological power is the use of statements that are nearly parallel. I say "nearly" because the matching phrases describe similar, but not identical, things:

- He is the firstborn over creation *and* He is the firstborn among the dead

- All things are created through Him, for Him *and* all things are reconciled in Him
- All things hold together in Him *and* He is the head of the church

The first half of each of these statements focuses on His preexistence and His role as Deity. The second half focuses on the work He did and does for the church in His role as God-man—claims that could not be made if He had not become human and completed His holy work.

IMAGE OF GOD (COL. 1:15)

Human beings were created in the image of God. Of course, the sin of Adam and Eve altered that image so greatly that all people are now naturally sinners. On our own, we don't resemble God anymore. Not so of Jesus: He was not born into sin. Even beyond that, however, He bears the image of God in a way no human could, not even our first parents. As Patzia says it, "Christ participates in and with the nature of God, not merely copying, but visibly manifesting and perfectly revealing God in human form."[2]

If you've ever had a bowl of ice milk or frozen yogurt, you know that it may be sweet and it may be cold, but it doesn't quite measure up to the creamy goodness of ice cream. (Perhaps a bit of personal opinion is mixed in here, but play along with me.) You can even buy your pretend ice cream in some of the same flavors as the real thing. It's a good substitute, perhaps, but most surely only a substitute. A believer in Christ is something like that—imitating the True One, but unable to completely represent Him. Christ, on the other hand, genuinely showed us God in that He *was* God. ("Anyone who has seen me has seen the Father" [John 14:9].) He represented all that God is, but He came to us in a mode that human beings could encounter without being overwhelmed.

FIRSTBORN OVER ALL CREATION (COL. 1:15)

For the modern reader, the expression *firstborn* seems to imply the first created being. In Scripture, however, it can be used to point to Christ as one with all authority. A child who was born first in the family had a position of privilege, of power. The phrase is helpful in this context not for portraying the second person of the Trinity as someone who had to be born, but for portraying Him as one who possessed the power and the rights of the Father, as a firstborn son would. The next verses make it clear that He was, in fact, not creat*ed*, but Creat*or*.

CHRIST THE CREATOR (COL. 1:16)

Probably every person living in the United States has seen a "bobblehead Jesus" at one time or another. I'm never quite sure who the makers had in mind as potential buyers. Were they designed for the faithful, so they can have a "fun" Jesus on the dashboard of their cars? Or are they intended for those who wish to blaspheme? Either way, it is still rather startling that such a trivial, ridiculous image has been made of the One who bears the full image of God and is Creator of all that exists. Jesus isn't "cute." He is omnipotent. He is sovereign. He is Creator.

One may wonder about the exclusion of the Father and the Holy Spirit when it comes to creating and governing the earth. If Christ has done all, what of the rest of the Trinity? The purpose here — indeed a major purpose of the entire book of Colossians — is to affirm the deity of Christ. The heresies running rampant in the Colossian church "falsified and depreciated the person and work of Christ."[3] Paul's praise of Christ doesn't mean that the Father and the Spirit aren't as critical; it is simply a means of emphasizing who Jesus really is. By establishing Him as Creator, he established Him as God.

As a person of the Trinity, Christ was absolutely involved in creation, and as Savior, He made human beings into new creations. This theme is consistent throughout the New

Testament. The original creation chose sin and destruction. Christ didn't come to redesign; He came to restore—to put all of earth and all of humanity as it was originally crafted to be. It is right and beautiful that the same One who originally created us in His image (see Gen. 1:27) is the One who restores us to our intended status as children of God and remakes us in His own image (see Rom. 8:29; 2 Cor. 3:18).

Verse 16 goes on to say that all things earthly and supernatural were created through Him and for Him (see also John 1:3).[4] Part of Paul's purpose in this statement was to debunk the Gnostic teaching that there were multiple cosmic spheres with varied levels of deities that ruled each one. Paul emphasized that there is one Creator, one Supreme Deity—not multiple gods at multiple levels. He wanted to make it clear that everything was created by Christ: heavenly and earthly things, visible and invisible things, thrones, powers, rulers, and authorities. This logically comes on the heels of his point in verse 15, that Jesus Christ is the image of the one true God. He is the one God and the Creator of all. All is created through Him and for Him, therefore "he must not be relegated to the same inferior position as other spiritual powers."[5] He is the cosmic ruler over all, and nothing exists unless He wills it.

We are less inclined to believe in multiple deities than the early Christians were. However, Paul's claims to the supremacy of Christ should still sear our hearts today.

When we get past looking at Jesus Christ as just our friend and have the maturity to regard Him as universal Lord, then we find ourselves humbled before Him and in a position of true worship.

ALL THINGS HOLD TOGETHER (COL. 1:17)

As I sat down to write today, I opened an email that broke my heart. A recovering addict who has been living in our church's post-rehabilitation transitional living apartments is back on the streets. I care about him and have spent much time working with him and for him. As I struggle with his poor choice, I again read the words, "In him all things hold together." But inwardly, I wonder, "Do they?"

"In him, everything is held together, protected, and prevented from disintegrating into chaos," reads one commentary.[6] The "everything" or "all things" of which this verse speaks, however, is the universe, the flow of life, the created order. In sustaining the universe, God does not infringe upon the free will of the people He has created. Human beings will do as they please, and sometimes that means that their lives disintegrate into chaos.

Those who place their lives in His hands and keep them there, however, can find great comfort in knowing that our Lord is Creator, Preserver, and Governor of this world.[7]

We can draw a line from His cosmic lordship to His involvement in the lives of those who seek to do His will. We can rest easy because "we know that in all things God works for the good of those who love him, who have been called according to his purpose" (Rom. 8:28). What an amazing thing it is to know that the God who holds the universe together holds our personal circumstances together when we live in submission to Him. Even our errors can be reworked into something good, and we can trust in His goodness when our hearts break for others.

THE SUPREME ONE (COL. 1:18)

Some of the ancient Greeks, such as Plato and Philo of Alexandria (closer to the time the New Testament was written) viewed the cosmos as something similar to a body or a uniform which required a head. The *eternal Logos*— the "Divine Word" as the Greeks understood it—or possibly even Zeus was the head of the body. As Paul moved from discussing the natural creation of Christ (the cosmos) to the new creation (the church and the people of whom it is comprised), it was fitting that he drew upon this metaphor.

For just as Christ is the head of all creation, so is He the head of the church body. The imagery of the body is also significant because Paul wanted the Colossians to understand that they were as much a part of this new faith movement as any Jew who came to believe in Christ. A body is a perfect illustration of multiple parts that must absolutely function together. Just as the mind in one's head commands all the functions of one's body, so our Head commands His body, His church.

In the second half of this verse we find Christ described as "the beginning" in most English translations. Unfortunately, this robs the original word, *archē,* of its full meaning. The word actually means "'first principle', 'source', 'creative initiative.'"[8] Paul was building a case as to why Christ is the Supreme One, so it is helpful to understand that when he called Christ "the beginning," he was calling Him the source and initiator of all things.

Not only did all things begin with Christ, they are reborn or remade because of Him. All that He had created was on a path toward death as a result of sin, but in the beautiful words of Romans 8:21, "creation itself will be liberated from its bondage to decay." Paul informs us that Christ is *firstborn* from the dead—which means that others will follow. *We* will follow. As He came back to life, so will we. Because Jesus Christ was the *archē* and because He is the firstborn amongst the dead, He is preeminent—supreme above all others.

FULLNESS OF GOD (COL. 1:19)

In verse 19, Paul directly addressed the Gnostic misunderstanding that many supernatural spheres existed between God and man, each one ruled by a different supernatural being. Those in the sphere closest to God were most deific; the closer the sphere was to the natural world, the less godlike its ruler would be. Paul said that it pleased God[9] to have *all His fullness* dwell in Christ. There is nothing in the middle. Christ is fully God, and all that He is walked among us.

Imagine what it must have been like for those who were physically in the presence of the One who had the fullness of God in Himself. Imagine Mary and Joseph, raising Him. Imagine the disciples, traveling with Him. Imagine the woman at the well, hearing Him declare Himself as the Messiah to her. Then remember what Jesus said,

Because you have seen me, you have believed; blessed are those who have not seen and yet have believed. (John 20:29)

That's us. We may wish we had been on this planet to experience Jesus in a visible, tangible way. But God has remembered us and blesses us for our faith. We bow before Christ with all believers of all generations, acknowledging who He truly is.

THE RECONCILER (COL. 1:20)

The glorious news is that Jesus was solely qualified to reconcile all things and has done so through His astonishing sacrifice. Scripture says that He has made peace with and reconciled all things to God. Legitimate questions have been raised as to the exact meaning of this. Has He reconciled all things of the cosmos, both physical and spiritual? Was our planet (the dirt, the trees, the oceans) lost from God because of sin, and is it now reconciled—or will it be in the future? Have the fallen angels been impacted by the blood of Christ?

This verse does not answer these questions. The point of this verse is that Christ is the reconciler, and He reconciles through His shed blood. Through no one else and through no other means can it be achieved.

REFLECTION QUESTIONS

1. What is the fuller meaning of the word *firstborn*, as explained in this study?

2. Why is Christ emphasized as the Creator in this passage?

3. What is the fuller meaning of the word *beginning* in this passage?

4. Most people would agree that our abuse of the earth has, at least to some degree, caused environmental problems. How does that square with the biblical truth that Christ holds everything together?

5. What things stand out to you as Paul built his case about who Jesus really is?

6. Would it impact the Christian faith if Jesus had been just a great prophet, and not the One who held the fullness of God? If so, how?

7. How has our society turned Jesus into something less than who He is? Have our churches also lost a sense of awe over who He truly is?

OUR NEW STATUS

COLOSSIANS 1:21–23

A friend of mine once questioned, "How can anyone consider a six-year-old a sinner?" My immediate thought was, "You must not know many six-year-olds." I'm the mother of five, and even before age six each one was quite recognizably a sinner!

At the age of seven, all of my children voluntarily signed a Junior Soldier Promise with The Salvation Army. It is a commitment to try to live a holy life that can be made after a course of preparatory study, and it identifies the child as an official part of our church body. The night before signing the promise, one of my children told a very big lie. I said, "Honey, you are going to be a Junior Soldier. When you sign the promise, it says that you will always tell the truth." To this my child responded, "What? I'm not signing that!"

Every human, past, present, and future—with the exception of One—has a shared experience: "All have sinned and fall short of the glory of God" (Rom. 3:23). As it says in Colossians 1:21, we were once enemies of God. Though each of us was born into a sinful state, we carried on sinning all on our own. In this passage, we will dig deeper into Paul's description of our spiritual "before and after," as God transforms our hearts as we move forward in faith.

FROM EVIL-MINDED ENEMIES (COL. 1:21)

When I was a teenager, my girlfriends and I tried to play a trick on some of our male friends. We made cupcakes and laced them with every inappropriate spice we could find in the cupboard—curry, celery salt, etc. When it was done, we covered them with vanilla frosting to make them as appealing as possible. The prank was unsuccessful, however. As soon as the boys lifted the cupcakes to their mouths, they got a whiff of those spices and knew they didn't want to take a bite.

Many enemies of God have sugar-frosted their lives. They do good deeds. They coach kids' sports or raise money to fight cancer or take meals to a sick workmate. But remember that those who are unsaved are still members of the dominion of darkness (1:13). Much like the spiced cupcakes, if you get close enough to them, you will notice that it is not the aroma of Christ you are smelling.

However, to say that unsaved individuals are at odds with God and that they practice evil behavior is not to say that they are incapable of any goodness at all. Some Christians are of the opinion that every good deed done by an unsaved person ultimately has a selfish (evil) motivation. For example, even if they anonymously put one hundred dollars in a Salvation Army kettle, that act made them feel good, so it was ultimately selfish. While you may find some truth to that, the reality is that many Christians are often guilty of the same thing.

The Wesleyan definition of *prevenient grace*—a measure of God's grace that infiltrates *every* life before salvation—teaches us that God has given all people a conscience. Because of that, unsaved people may do truly good things without selfish motive.[1] But righteously motivated deeds mixed with selfishly motivated deeds are not enough to reconcile us to God. Despite a veritably good act, "there is no one righteous, not even one" (Rom. 3:10).

Verse 21 also says that we were enemies in our minds because of our evil behavior. Many of us, however, think that the reverse is true: the mind is evil and the behavior follows suit. It's almost a chicken-or-egg scenario. Was the mind evil first, or the behavior? It really doesn't matter. The point is that we were at odds with God. And this is why, in the depths of our beings, all of us feel a sense of unrest until we come to Christ. Within every unsaved person there is discord. We are not what we are made to be when we are the foes of God rather than the children of God.

TO RECONCILED PEOPLE (COL. 1:22)

Only the bodily death of Christ could turn us from enemies into holy children of God. In the previous study we talked about Gnosticism, one of the heresies that threatened the Colossian church. Gnosticism taught that flesh was evil, so it was unthinkable that God would become flesh. From this idea flowed Docetism, the teaching that Jesus was *not* flesh, but merely appeared to be—that He was something like a phantom. Paul emphasized here that Christ had a physical body that suffered death. No mere pantomime of death would clear our sins. Jesus bore great suffering and His body was verified as dead when a soldier pierced His side and blood and water flowed out. How vast is God's love, that He should become mortal and die the most gruesome death of all to reunite humanity with Himself!

Though none of us were alive at the time of the death of Christ, it was at that moment that Christ atoned for the sins of the world. The power of His saving work reached both into the past and the future. The ancient Jews before Christ had sacrificed animals as a placeholder for the coming sacrifice of the true Lamb of God. These sacrifices cleared their sins because they represented the coming salvation through Christ. For us, our salvation began at the cross, though we had yet to be born.

Lyricist Elisha Albright Hoffman wrote:

Down at the cross where my Savior died,
Down where for cleansing from sin I cried,
There to my heart **was** the blood applied,
Glory to His name!

Glory to His name, glory to His name!
Now to my heart **is** the blood applied,
Glory to His name![2]

Note the past/present tense application of the blood of Christ (bold font mine). Or consider the words of the old spiritual: "Were you there when they crucified my Lord?" Of course you weren't there—and yet, you were, in the sense that that was the moment of your salvation, even though you didn't receive Christ for many, many years after that. This thought is worth contemplating because it reflects upon the cosmic power of Christ that is unbound by the limits of time. It also gives us opportunity to use holy imagination, to see ourselves present at the foot of the cross, knowing that we bore guilt for His suffering. Stuart Townend penned these words:

Behold the Man upon a cross,
My sin upon His shoulders;
Ashamed, I hear my mocking voice
Call out among the scoffers.
It was my sin that held Him there,
Until it was accomplished;
His dying breath has brought me life—
I know that it is finished.[3]

And if the human status of Christ wasn't too limiting, perhaps He even thought of each of us on the day He gave His life. Perhaps the name of everyone who would willingly choose Him went through His head, giving Him strength for the horrific task.

HOLY IN HIS SIGHT (COL. 1:22)

Continuing on in verse 22 we read that the death of Christ results in us being presented holy in God's sight. As a Wesleyan, when I see the word *holy,* bells and whistles go off in my head. We have a beautiful teaching within our tradition, one that those of other doctrinal persuasions sometimes find too presumptuous. I find it utterly hopeful. It is the teaching that because we have put to death the "old man" within us and allowed the Holy Spirit to reign over our lives, we have the capacity to always choose obedience over sin. There is *never* a time when we are powerless and must default to sin! We always have the potential for victorious living because we are indeed reconciled children of God.

That is not to say, however, that we reach a point where we no longer need to be molded and shaped. We continue to grow in holiness because God continues to reveal to us the sharp edges of our character that we didn't previously recognize. Our attainable hope is to be submitted to God in every known area of our lives. But God will never stop revealing more segments of ourselves, unknown flawed areas, and we submit them to Him as we learn of them.[4]

Colossians 1:33 speaks of another facet of holiness, and that is a conferred status. When we leave this life and meet the Lord, all sin—intentional and unintentional—will cease to be part of our being. We will be presented to God as blameless. In the meantime, though we are still learning how to live holy lives, we have the word *holy* stamped across our foreheads—God has granted us that status. The writings of Paul are full of what is called "already and not yet" theology. We live in between what exists and what is certain for the future. We are already seen as completely holy, even though our holiness is not yet fully realized.

Believers progress in their relationships with Christ. Hardly a person is converted who *immediately* lives a holy life as described above. And some Christians really never get to that stage of full submission within their lifetimes. As N. T. Wright explained:

God's purpose, then, is to create a holy people in Christ. This he *has* done in principle, by dealing with sin on the cross and thus already achieving reconciliation. This he *is* doing in practice, by refashioning their lives according to the pattern of the perfect life, that of Christ (see 3:10). This he *will* do in the future, when that work is complete and the church enjoys fully that which at present it awaits in hope.[5]

ESTABLISHED IN FAITH (COL. 1:23)

Remember that Paul was speaking to a group of new Christians who were experiencing an onslaught of heresy. In this verse, his warning was to continue in the pure teachings of the gospel as opposed to a faith diluted by heresy.

The words "established and firm" refer to the structure of a building, specifically the security of its foundation and superstructure. Repeated earthquakes had taken a devastating toll on the city of Colossae (see introduction). The Colossians could probably look around them and see how buildings with fine foundations and framework had survived, and those that had been built carelessly did not. Only a faith whose foundations and framework were built upon "the hope held out in the gospel" could last.

If the Colossians allowed the heresies that surrounded them to become part of the basic structure of their belief system, they would not be building a faith that could survive. They would not be continuing in the gospel faith that had been taught to them. Should that happen, they would not be presented among the holy and blameless, reconciled people of God.

I find two implications for us today. First, it is our duty to see that the gospel message taught in our believing bodies remains pure. Like the Colossians, we must be on guard against heretical teachings of all kinds. We also must be on our guard against secularism, which easily slithers into any fissures in our faith and splits it apart. To keep our faith whole and healthy we must thoroughly understand the gospel and be unreservedly committed to it. We must do this as a united people of Christ.

The second implication is more individual. Those who walk away from the faith they once received have rejected all that was freely given to them. The promise of verse 22 is conditional: We are reconciled through Christ and presented as free from accusation *if* we continue in our faith. It is amazing how tempted we are to stomp off, away from God, because life isn't going the way we want it to. If we really try to wrap our minds around the sacrifice that has been made for us, we realize that it is absurd for us to be angry about what has or hasn't happened, what we did or didn't get, or what someone else's situation is compared to ours— the complaints that usually lead people to abandon Christ.

EVERYBODY'S GOSPEL (COL. 1:23)

When Paul wrote that the gospel had been "proclaimed to every creature under heaven" he was using a little poetic license. His point was not that all living things had heard the good news of Jesus. We know that wasn't true. Rather, he was underscoring his previous point that the gospel was for all people, not for just one nation nor for selected individuals. The Gnostics taught that only certain people were given special knowledge from God and the rest were left out. Here, Paul punched another hole in heretical doctrine.

Over the past few centuries and even today there are many churches that understand Scripture to say that God has elected some people to be saved and has not elected others. Let us find comfort in Paul's message here: the gospel is for everyone. Christ's sacrifice brings limitless grace! It was not a partial atonement for the sins of a select few. He did not pour His love on one segment of His creation and turn His back on the rest. Here are glorious words penned by John Bakewell:

Hail, Thou once despisèd Jesus
Hail, Thou Galilean King!
Thou didst suffer to release us;
Thou didst free salvation bring.
Hail, thou universal Savior,
Bearer of our sin and shame!
By Thy merits we find favor;
Life is given through Thy name.[6]

REFLECTION QUESTIONS

1. Do you remember doing things from a pure conscience before you were saved? (Or, if you were saved as a young child, do you think you've seen examples in others of a pure conscience?) What role do you think prevenient grace played in your unselfish motivation?

2. Can you think of an area in your life in which evil thoughts have affected or are currently affecting your behavior?

3. What sort of false teaching or worldly attitudes try to infiltrate the church today? How do we protect against them?

4. Describe in your own words the sacrifice Christ made to reconcile humanity to God.

5. How has God been refining you lately? Are you aware of any area of your life that is not submitted to God?

6. What things in your life have made you angry at God? How have you handled that?

THE MYSTERY PROCLAIMED

COLOSSIANS 1:24–29

We've all had those moments where we've said to a friend or family member, "Who would have thought we'd end up here?" About ten years ago my family went on vacation to Alexandria, Virginia and Washington, DC. We had a grand time and fell in love with the area. One of my favorite moments of that trip was when we stopped at a park on the George Washington Parkway and got stuck in an unexpected rainstorm. The boys danced around, getting thoroughly soaked, and we laughed and laughed. Little did we know that two years later The Salvation Army would transfer us across the country to Alexandria! I couldn't have imagined that I would pass that park nearly every day as I drove to work.

I'm reminded of that when I sense Paul's wonder at the revelation of the mystery of Christ, which we will explore in more detail in this study.

SOMETHING LACKING? (COL. 1:24)

Many verses in the Bible leave us scratching our heads, and verse 24 is certainly one of them. Here, Paul seemed to imply that the sacrifice of Christ was not enough and that somehow, through Paul's own suffering, *he* made up for what was "still lacking." However, throughout all of his epistles Paul unequivocally taught that "all are justified freely by his grace through the redemption that came by Christ Jesus" (Rom. 3:24). Nothing could or should be added to what Jesus has done to provide salvation.

So what was Paul talking about when he said, ". . . fill up in my flesh what is still lacking in regard to Christ's afflictions, for the sake of his body, which is the church"? Indeed, Paul had suffered and was still suffering, but how did that fill any gaps for the sake of the church? How could Paul even suggest that there could be any gaps in the atoning work of Christ? Bible scholars have come up with varied attempts to make sense of this verse. Here are a few of the ideas:

- **Paul was referring to what is known as the "Messianic woes."**[1] The Jewish people believed in two separate ages: the age before the Messiah, and the age after the Messiah came to reign. They believed that the people who awaited the Messiah—the true children of God—would suffer greatly as the old age faded away and the new age began. Since this would have been familiar teaching to Paul, he may well have viewed the period between Jesus' ascension and His return to earth as the overlap between the old age and the new one. Jesus had started the new age, but it wouldn't have fully arrived until Jesus returned ("already and not yet" theology). So, Paul and the other followers of Jesus would be in the waiting stage, characterized by suffering for true believers.

- **Paul was in mystical union with Christ.**[2] This connectedness meant that Paul's sufferings for the church could be regarded as though they were experienced by Christ Himself.

- **Paul was speaking of something *he himself* lacked, not Christ.**[3] Reread the verse with that in mind. Perhaps he was implying that through suffering, he was being made more complete, more like Christ, in his own sufferings. This theory seems to be the most palatable.

Though we cannot be certain what Paul meant in this verse, we can know beyond all doubt that the blood shed by our Lord Jesus Christ was more than enough for the task of atoning for our sin. The One in whom the fullness of God dwelled did not need help from any human in completing the work of salvation.

THE MYSTERY (COL. 1:25–27)

It had been known that God would have some sort of provision of grace for the Gentiles. For generations, there had been "God-fearers"—Gentiles who accepted and worshiped the Hebrew God. But who would have thought that Jews and Gentiles would be united as one body through the Messiah? Who could have predicted that? It seems obvious to us now, but this had been the "mystery that has been kept hidden for ages and generations."

F. F. Bruce observed, "The saving purpose of God was a major theme of the OT prophets, and that Gentiles as well as Israelites were embraced within its scope was also foreseen. But the manner in which that purpose would come to fruition—by the incorporation of Gentile and Jewish believers alike in the common life of the body of Christ—was not made known."[4]

Wright also points out that God's glory is to be shared with His people, and the people to whom Paul wrote were guaranteed to be part of that, because they belonged to Christ.[5] In this way, Christ in them (the great mystery) is the hope of glory. And the mystery is as great riches; think how much poorer salvation would be if it only included the Jews, or if the Gentiles were viewed as foster children to God, sort of one step removed, while the Jews were His "real" children. Instead they (we) are fully adopted into the family and share the rights and privileges of the initial family members (the Jews).

Paul was clearly delighted with the union of Jews and Gentiles in the body of Christ. He used the theme in other epistles, and he evidenced a feeling of kinship toward the Colossian people in this chapter. He rejoiced in suffering for the church (v. 24) and made Himself its servant (v. 25). He considered the union of Jews and Gentiles in the body of Christ to be the "fullness" of the word of God. Again, it meant that the gospel is not lean, not poor, not partial. Our God is completely capable and every bit willing to provide hope for every human being He has created and will create. He is *mighty* to save.

PROCLAIMING IT (COL. 1:28–29)

Paul and his coworkers (including Epaphras) proclaimed Christ, then instructed and corrected believers so that they might become *teleios* in Christ. *Teleios* can be translated as perfect, mature, or complete. As no one will ever be perfect in every way in this lifetime, only through the blood of Christ are we given that status. It is a label we wear, though it is undeserved. It has been conferred upon us. (See the previous study, verse 22.)

However, in verses 28 and 29, Paul talked about working toward making the people *teleios*. He and his colleagues were "admonishing and teaching everyone with all wisdom." He was working "strenuously" toward this goal. So, Paul is not speaking of the kind of *teleios* that is conferred upon us with no effort made. We must do the work involved in growing into mature people of God. Paul attested to "the energy Christ so powerfully works in me." Without the strength Christ supplies, we cannot mature. But this does not mean we sit back and become mature by doing nothing. We must take deliberate action toward our maturity, and receiving wise instruction and correction is part of that endeavor.

According to the Gnostics, *teleios* was possible for the chosen ones who had received a special knowledge from God, not accessible to everyone. But Paul was laboring so that everyone might become mature in Christ. Again, the theme is that within Christ there is equality. All can be saved. All can become mature. The only distinction that remains is between those who are willing and those who are not.

REFLECTION QUESTIONS

1. How do you feel when you read verses that are hard to interpret, such as verse 24?

2. Which of the three theories on verse 24 seems to be the best explanation in your opinion? Why?

3. What is the mystery Paul explains, and does it have anything to do with your life?

4. How is God currently working in your life to make you more mature?

7

TOGETHER IN LOVE.
TOGETHER IN DOCTRINE.

COLOSSIANS 2:1–5

In 2017, I spent six weeks in England attending a personal spiritual growth/educational event for Salvation Army officers—thirty-three of us from around the world. My deskmate was from India. My reflection group included people from Australia, Burundi, South Africa, Romania, and the United States. I shared laughs with friends from Japan, Canada, and Mexico. We had cultural nights when people danced native dances and wore traditional costumes. We sampled treats from their homelands. (I dressed as a cowgirl with some other North Americans and taught the kitchen staff to prepare s'mores!) More than once we sang this well-known Salvation Army song:

They shall come from the east,
They shall come from the west,

And sit down in the Kingdom of God;
To be met by their Father
And welcomed and blessed,
And sit down in the Kingdom of God.
The black, the white, the dark, the fair,
Your color will not matter there;
They shall come from the east,
They shall come from the west,
And sit down in the Kingdom of God.[1]

The third verse of that song has these words:

From every tribe and every race,
All men as brothers shall embrace.

While I was enjoying all of this diversity, learning from
and loving my brothers and sisters from around the world, a
young woman in Virginia was killed when someone intentionally struck her with his car because she was protesting against
a white supremacist/neo-Nazi rally. As a mixed-raced woman
with two adopted children who are fully black, I was shaken
and a bit frightened. I was also struck by the stark contrast
between what I was experiencing at my event in the United
Kingdom and what was happening in my home country.

Prejudice is nothing new. Jews such as Paul had been
raised with significant prejudice against non-Jews. In the

previous study I explored the fact that, while Jews had known there would be some provision of salvation for non-Jewish God-fearers, no one had expected Jews and Gentiles to be united together as they now were in Christ. I think they had anticipated more of a "separate but equal" situation.

Beginning in the late nineteenth century and on into the mid-twentieth, the demands of the Fourteenth Amendment of the American Constitution were considered legally met when people were separated by race as long as blacks and whites received "equal" services in housing, education, employment, etc. Of course, the services were unilaterally inferior for blacks, and sometimes even nonexistent. They were separate, all right, but not equal.

Similarly, the Jewish people would have expected some other means, some secondary method of salvation for the Gentiles. And they probably wouldn't have complained if it wasn't quite as beautiful as the plan God had for the nation of Israel. But the great mystery had been revealed: Jews and Gentiles were saved by the same blood and brought together corporately in Christ. We will explore this mystery in depth in this passage of Colossians.

UNITY (COL. 2:1–2)

Before Christ intervened in Paul's (Saul's) life, he cherished his Jewish pedigree, which made him "superior" to Gentiles and even to many Jews. What a change occurred in his heart! Now he struggled on behalf of the new Christians in Colossae and Laodicea and others whom he had never even met—Gentiles, all. He wanted them to live in unity, to understand the mystery of their salvation, and to achieve spiritual maturity. For this, he was willing to be put in chains (4:3).

Any sinful stronghold can be pulverized through the power of Christ. One of those strongholds is prejudice. Christians are meant to be "united in love." We share salvation, and we are mystically brought together as the shared body of Christ, with Him as the holy head. No space exists for racial prejudice, gender prejudice, nor any other kind of prejudice within the body of Christ; a body functions as a unit and loves itself.

As Paul wrote in 1 Corinthians 12:25, "There should be no division in the body, . . . its parts should have equal concern for each other." Brenda Salter McNeil expresses it this way:

"On the cross Jesus reconciled us to God, and he also reconciled us to each other—both in the same act of salvation. Because of the death and resurrection of Jesus Christ, there are no divisions or barriers that separate us from God or from each other. To choose Christ is also to choose his community.[2]

This life of unity is one of the hallmarks of spiritual maturity. In 1:28–29, Paul "strenuously contended" so that the Christians might be mature (*teleios*). In 2:1–2 Paul said that he was "contending" with the goal that the Christians be encouraged and unified. Maturity is characterized by an uplifted spirit and a willingness to live in unity with others.

One of the comments on a child's report card might read, "Doesn't play well with others." Children often don't. Those who refuse to work together and live in harmony are notably immature. To be mature means to understand give and take, generosity, and selflessness.

THE SOURCE OF THE MYSTERY (COL. 2:2–3)

In the previous chapter Paul said that the mystery of God was "Christ in you" (1:27). Here he says that the mystery is Christ Himself. To make an issue over this would really be splitting hairs. Christ is the agent of salvation; His intervention in people's lives, and especially in the lives of Gentiles, was the working out of the mystery. And therefore, in Him "are hidden all the treasures of wisdom and knowledge."

Only the true God could possess all wisdom and knowledge. The first chapter of Colossians leave no doubt that Christ is that true God. Everything is found in Him. Everything originates from Him. Patzia writes: "There is no need for the Colossians to look beyond Christ; there is no purpose in pursuing other systems of thought; there is no value in secret initiations. Christ is all and in him are all things!"[3]

Whatever heresies sought to entangle the Colossians, they could roll them into a pile and toss the whole thing away. We may not be beset by the same heresies today, but we can rejoice that the Savior we worship is the eternal God and the source of all that is true and right.

UNFLAPPABLE (COL. 2:4–5)

Fortunately, the heresies had not yet won the hearts and minds of the Colossians. In verse 4 Paul warned them against slick philosophies that would tickle their ears. They had not succumbed, but Paul knew this would be an area of vulnerability for the Colossians.

We are well aware that physical drives and emotional needs can provide great targets for the enemy. The need for physical touch can bloom into lust. The desire for relationship can morph into jealousy. We can fall prey to assaults on our minds, as well. A healthy desire to be open-minded, for example, can stray into a rejection of the Word of God. Jesus told us to love God with all our heart, soul, mind, and strength, and all of these are critical because all of them form who we are as human beings. But we must guard against what sounds right but doesn't come from God. We are blessed because we have something the Colossians didn't have: the canonized Scripture to guide us.

While heresy loomed about the Colossians, Paul praised them for their "orderliness" and "steadfastness" (2:5 MEV).[4] These words were military terms and may have been used to evoke the image of strong soldiers for Christ. I surmise that they kept their collective doctrine in order and checked up on one another's adherence to the doctrine. They seem to have been an unflappable congregation, and Paul wanted it to stay that way.

My husband and I had been pastoring our church for about two years when one of the people who had attended for decades approached me. She was having trouble with a basic, nonnegotiable Christian doctrine. I admired and greatly appreciated her bravery in opening discussion with me. However, I was troubled to think that she had sat in more Bible studies and heard more sermons than she could count but had never understood this foundational biblical truth. She wasn't even convinced it was true.

All Christians of reasonable maturity should be nurturing and helping the less experienced. My teenage son was surprised to learn that a "tween" boy at our church admired him greatly. He realized he had some responsibility to model Christian faith and perhaps even to mentor that boy. The Lord expects us to lead each other in this way. Being orderly in our faith means that we take care to be sure everyone in our faith family understands what we believe. This is a big job. But we must remember that discipleship and teaching are not the work of pastors or corps officers alone.

REFLECTION QUESTIONS

1. Why is prejudice so much at odds with the New Testament view of the church?

2. Buddhism, Islam, Hinduism and other religious sects have kernels of truth in them. How do you square with the idea that all wisdom and knowledge are hidden in Christ?

3. What secular philosophies or incorrect religious theories have you encountered?

4. Are there any basic Christian beliefs with which you struggle? Is there anyone who can help you sort them out?

5. Is anyone feeding into your spiritual life personally? Are you (or should you be) feeding into anyone else's?

8

SO THEN

COLOSSIANS 2:6–8

Remember being in school and learning to write a thesis statement? It was the main point of your essay curled up tightly into one or two sentences. The rest of the essay rolled out the details. Although we are already into the second chapter of Colossians, we now see Paul's thesis statement: "So then, just as you received Christ Jesus as Lord, continue to live your lives in him." The reason Paul wrote the book was that the Colossians might grow in their faith and rebuke heresy. They were to understand and claim their new identity in Christ and to live accordingly. They were to understand the identity of Christ Himself (His Lordship) and reject any false teaching about Him.

CONTINUE TO LIVE YOUR LIFE IN HIM (COL. 2:6–7)

There is a woman on social media who regularly gives people advice on how to be healthy. Initially I was willing to read what she had to say because she had gone from chunky to thin and posted lots of pictures of herself working out or participating in a 5K run. She was inspirational. Over time, however, she continued to give advice as she packed on weight. She didn't seem to be working out anymore, and one could assume she had probably let her diet regimen slip as well. She ceased to be a role model to me, and she didn't seem to be doing herself much good either.

Most positive changes in life require vigilance. Paul reminded us to continue to live our lives in Christ. I have seen many people kneel at the altar to accept Christ as Savior. Unfortunately, some of them put effort into living a Christian life for a while, but grow weary of the effort it requires. They don't want to actually change the way they've been living. Many of these people still claim to be Christian, but their lives give no indication of it. Making Christ Lord of our lives means relinquishing control to Him, thoroughly and permanently.

Why do some people have such a loose grasp on the idea of Christ being Lord of our lives? Why do they cease to continue in obedience to Him? Verse 7 requires that we be "rooted and built up . . . strengthened in the faith as you were taught." Again, this requires vigilance. These things do not happen when Scripture, involvement in church body life, and Christian disciplines take a backseat to other priorities. In Jesus' parable of the sower's seed (see Matt. 13:2–9), only the seeds that encountered receptive soil flourished. Receptive soil allows roots to grow and the plant to grow in strength. It involves time and maintenance.

OVERFLOWING WITH THANKFULNESS (COL. 2:7)

Paul reminded us to be thankful in verse 7. Perhaps we should consider how thank*less* it is to take the good news of the Lord crucified and mix it with other faiths. The only appropriate response to a Lord who is both sacrificial and mighty is to live as described:

- Rooted and built up in Him
- Strengthened in the faith
- Overflowing with thankfulness
- Unsusceptible to human tradition and the elemental spiritual forces of this world

PHILOSOPHY, TRADITION, AND SPIRITUAL FORCES (COL. 2:8)

Paul did not specify what philosophy might lead the Colossians astray. He did not have an issue with philosophy in general.[1] Philosophy means "love of wisdom"—not a bad thing. But the concern was that believers would replace "Christ, in whom are hidden all the treasures of wisdom and knowledge" (2:2–3) with the wisdom of the world.

Paul actually broadened the word *philosophy* in this verse by referring to human tradition and spiritual forces of the world. His concerns seemed to range from traditional Greek philosophy to pagan religious practices (such as the worship of earth, air, fire, and water—the "elemental spiritual forces") to Jewish traditions being forced upon Christian converts.

Requiring commitment to Jewish law for those under the gospel of Christ was a common problem for early Christians, and it was rather nonsensical. The law was the placeholder for the Savior. Christ *was* that Savior. So, to obligate converts to practice what had to be done in anticipation of Him while living within the freedom of the gospel seemed to evidence an uncertainty that Christ really was who He claimed to be.

And that—underestimating who Christ really is—is really the fundamental issue, perhaps both then and now.

Compared to Him, all else is hollow at best, and deceptive at worst. That is because Christ *is* God. Who or what deserves equal worship? Who or what else deserves our devotion and our gratitude?

HERESIES (COL. 2:8)

Much of Colossians 1 was spent exploring the glory of the Lord Jesus. This doctrinal foundation was crucial. If the people did not understand who Christ truly was—His glory, His deity, His power to resurrect—they would be vulnerable to false teachings. They had received the true gospel from Epaphras and were to continue establishing themselves in that truth; namely, that Christ Jesus is Lord. As children of God and holders of the "mystery," they were to flourish in that truth, growing into mature believers (which we will dive into in Colossians 3).

Paul also made reference to certain heresies the people had heard, most specifically Gnosticism/Docetism, and perhaps a bit of Jewish mysticism (see introduction). But here in Colossians 2, he began taking aim at the syncretic blend of Jewish law with faith in Christ. His language became quite strong in verse 8. The verb that is translated "takes you captive" in the NIV actually has the meaning of carrying off the believers as booty.[2]

To mash up gospel truth with human philosophy or Hellenistic Judaism was to push Christ to the side, favoring the enslavement of human tradition and "elemental spiritual forces of the world"—a phrase which could mean something demonic or could be a reference to the false gods that others worshiped.

Even today in certain countries, syncretism (the mixing of different belief systems) leads people far from the things Christ taught us. Christians worship their ancestors or practice voodoo in some parts of the world, mixing human tradition and elemental spiritual forces with gospel truth. In the Western world, we don't see much of that. But we do see human philosophies being stirred into Christian doctrine and creating an erroneous mess. For example, the phrase "God helps those who help themselves" bears no resemblance to any scriptural notion, yet there are many who think it is gospel truth and live by it. Rather than humbling themselves before the Lord first, they seek to do things on their own strength.

Facebook alone is full of Christians who post a thought from Eastern philosophy one day and a thought from the Bible the next. That is not to say that every Eastern philosophical thought is completely wrong. But sometimes they are. In fact, they are quite often in direct contradiction to the Bible. But people who have let their spiritual armor drop don't see the issue.

In many environments a person is better received if she makes space for all religions. Those who tout Dalai Lama one day, Mohammed the next, and Jesus the day after that may come across as big-hearted and nonjudgmental. Enlightened, even. But this is the hollow and deceptive way of the world. Note that verse 6 talks about receiving Christ as *Lord*. He is not only the one who has saved us, He is supposed to be the indisputable master of our lives. None other can stand beside Him. No words of wisdom or truth are comparable to His. He is the source and origin of all that is—He is in a class by Himself both universally and in the heart of each Christian.

REFLECTION QUESTIONS

1. What is syncretism, and how do you see it in our culture?

2. Are you making an effort to be rooted and built up in Christ?

3. Verse 7 says we are to overflow with thankfulness. Make a list of ten things you are thankful for.

4. Write or speak a prayer in which you acknowledge to Christ your understanding of who He really is.

9

MORE THAN A MAN

COLOSSIANS 2:9–10

You can find many varying stories about the origin of the phrase "the real McCoy." One of those stories concerns the invention of a man named Elijah McCoy. Son of escaped slaves, he was a prolific inventor best known for his creation of an oil-drip cup used by railroad companies. This device was effective and saved money, so other inventors tried to create knockoff versions to get in on the action. Because the knockoffs were inferior, train engineers would often ask whether locomotives were equipped with "the real McCoy."

The human philosophies and traditions mentioned in the last study were the knockoffs that people had used to replace the true God. But Jesus was the real McCoy, leaving any other philosophy or tradition in the dust. Verse 9 leaves no room for waffling on that point. And, to carry the illustration of the oil-drip cup to its obvious end, those who equip their lives with a relationship with "the real McCoy" are able to fulfill their function and live a better life than those who settle for the imitation.

THE IDENTITY OF CHRIST (COL. 2:9)

The claim in verse 9 is a restatement of 1:19. It bore repeating because the identity of Christ can be neither misunderstood nor compromised. Here we find the surprising and unique revelation of Christianity: that God would become human and dwell among us, and Jesus of Nazareth was that human embodiment. He was not like the divine humans that the Greeks believed in. He was the *fullness of all Deity*, taking on the form of a human.

As Christianity spread and time progressed, whole generations—whole centuries of generations—were born into families and cultures that had already embraced this concept, particularly in the Western world. A shift, however, began to occur in the late nineteenth and early twentieth centuries and continues to this day. Many began to identify Jesus as a prophet or good man, but not as a member of the Godhead. In *Mere Christianity,* C. S. Lewis famously balked at such theories:

I am trying here to prevent anyone saying the really foolish thing that people often say about Him: "I'm ready to accept Jesus as a great moral teacher, but I don't accept His claim to be God." That is the one thing we must not say. A man who was merely a man and said the sort of things Jesus said would not be a great moral teacher. He would either be a lunatic — on a level with the man who says he is a poached egg — or else he would be the Devil of Hell. You must make your choice. Either this man was, and is, the Son of God: or else a madman or something worse. You can shut Him up for a fool, you can spit at Him and kill Him as a demon; or you can fall at His feet and call Him Lord and God. But let us not come up with any patronising nonsense about His being a great human teacher. He has not left that open to us. He did not intend to.[1]

If we relegate Christ to some status other than Lord and Savior, then our faith no longer makes sense. His teachings would be based on false claims and His sacrificial death would not be enough to cover our sins because He would be a flawed human, like we are. And, as Lewis points out, He would be either crazy to have made the claims He did, or a cruel deceiver. Our salvation hinges on the fact that Jesus is the Holy Son of God, second member of the Trinity.

As Salvation Army doctrine states, the Father, Son and Holy Spirit are "undivided in essence and co-equal in power and glory."[2]

BROUGHT TO FULLNESS (COL. 2:10)

Because Jesus was (and is) Deity in bodily form, we are "brought to fullness." I have known more than a few people who struggle with drug addiction. Addiction causes people to waste away physically; you can see it right before your eyes. Some of the most visible changes in health are seen in those addicted to "meth" (crystal methamphetamine). They lose massive amounts of weight. Their teeth rot and eventually fall out. I've seen men and women in their twenties who look like they are in their sixties thanks to meth.

I've had the joy, however, of seeing meth addicts get clean. Their skin actually brightens. They put on some much-needed weight. Several I've known decided to get dentures and began to smile freely again. They move from a state of decay to a state of vigor. Similarly, before being in Christ, a person is withering due to sin. We are born sinners, and we seem to grow progressively worse. We find our pet sins, and we work on perfecting them. As a result, we spiritually waste away. But when we come to Christ, we are "brought to fullness." We are characterized by spiritual vitality as He restores us to what was originally intended when He created humankind. That is to say, He progressively restores us to His own image.

This could not be achieved in our lives through the teachings and martyrdom of a good prophet. A prophet might influence the way we think and even some of our behavior. But no prophet could completely restore us, bringing us around to what we were meant to be. This is the work of a Savior alone, and only a Savior of deific status is qualified for the job.

OVER EVERY POWER AND AUTHORITY (COL. 2:10)

Christ is the head over every power and authority. His role as the master of the universe has been firmly established already in Colossians. Verse 1:17, for example, told us that "in him all things hold together." Despite all the discordance in our world, we may notice that it hasn't fallen apart. And we are aware that someday Christ will return and all humanity, living and dead, will bow before Him as Lord.

But perhaps we can take a more personal meaning from this verse. Because we have found our fullness in Him, we have no place else to turn for fulfillment. Just as He is over every power and authority in His role as Lord of the universe, so is He over every power and authority that would seek to influence our lives. Our hope, our salvation, and personal direction for our lives—it is all in Him.

Many sincere people believe that they should pray to different saints depending on their needs. But this practice seems to be akin to an employee at a corporation taking his complaints to his manager rather than marching straight into the office of the CEO. Through His barrier-breaking work, Christ gave us the right to approach Him directly. We are told to "approach God's throne of grace with confidence" (Heb. 4:16).

The two youngest children in our family were adopted from another country, where they had previously lived in poverty and fear. For a long time, the older of the two was terrified to ask for anything. He would often either expect his sister to meet his need or he would sway her to petition us on his behalf. As parents, this was painful for us. We wanted him to understand that we were the people of power in his life, not his little sister. We had the resources he needed, and as parents we were the ones with authority and control. We also wanted him to know that he was free to come to us with any need and even with his desires, because we loved him. It was our hearts' desire that he should understand that he was valued and safe and that he could trust his parents.

In the same way, the Lord Jesus wants us to understand that because He is the ultimate power and authority in this world, He is able to care for us. He is Lord and Master of the universe, and He is the Good Shepherd to each of His sheep. Could we be in a more privileged position?

REFLECTION QUESTIONS

1. Do you agree with C. S. Lewis that Jesus couldn't possibly be just a great moral teacher? Why or why not?

2. Who do you think is the most powerful human on the planet? List some areas where that person's power cannot reach, but Christ's can. (For example, the powerful person cannot control the weather, but the Lord Himself has set weather patterns in motion.)

3. Describe the identity of Christ in your own words.

4. Is there an area in your life right now where you need to remind yourself of God's power and authority?

10

OUR NEW IDENTITY

COLOSSIANS 2:11–13

The identity of an individual is forever altered when he or she confesses Christ. In fact, the change is so monumental that believers are described as having died with Christ, been buried, and risen again in the strength of God. If we are to live truly free, sanctified lives, we must wrap our heads around what a dramatic work Christ has done in us. We must understand that we are indeed new creations.

Even those who got saved in their kindergarten Sunday school class experienced a wondrous transformation because they were "rescued . . . from the dominion of darkness" and brought into "the kingdom of the Son" (Col. 1:13). We don't like to think of unsaved children as little sinners running around. But the fact is that all of us were born into sin, and the trajectory of our lives was selfish and ungodly until we allowed Christ to intervene, no matter how old we were or how complicated our sins were or were not. It is a mistake to discount the power of salvation in the lives of the very young. Born sons and daughters of Adam, we were each possessed by the dark desire to be our own god. To be redeemed and made sons and daughters of the new Adam (Christ) is to abandon the dark and run into the Sonlight. It is the beginning of new life and new identity.

THE CIRCUMCISION (COL. 2:11)

As a Salvation Army officer, I consider the Salvation Army uniform to be a very positive thing. I have had strangers who recognized my uniform approach me and ask for prayer or some sort of spiritual guidance. Most people don't recognize the uniform, however, and I have had Spirit-led conversations that began by somebody asking me what branch of the military I was in or for which airline I worked.

I became a Salvation Army soldier when I was a teenager, which first gave me the opportunity to wear the uniform. I took great pride in it. It never occurred to me that wearing it might be considered embarrassing. But one day, a fellow young Salvationist and I were in public in our uniforms when my friend shrieked and pulled me in front of her. It turned out she had spotted a classmate and was wholly mortified at the thought of being seen in that uniform.

The uniform itself says much. It identifies members of a universal group of people dedicated to God and to humankind. It is a symbol meant to broadcast the conviction of the person wearing it. But if the heart of the wearer isn't committed to its uncompromising message and the bold declaration of the same, the uniform is just a weird-looking outfit, and maybe even a source of embarrassment.

Not unlike the uniform, Jewish circumcision identified males as members of God's elect. Under the old covenant, just undergoing the procedure was enough for inclusion. Traditional circumcision was performed upon a boy child eight days after birth, so it had nothing to do, of course, with the will of the child. Rather, it was the parents' obedience to Mosaic law.

The circumcision by Christ (or *of* Christ, depending on your translation) also identifies a person as one of the elect, but it requires the will of the individual. The point Paul was making was that external acts—rituals, if you will—hold no meaning in and of themselves under the new covenant. The person must be in earnest. The old practice was done because it was customary. It certainly held no meaning in the heart and mind of the eight-day-old baby!

In this passage Paul used the word "circumcision" in an unusual way. You can interpret it in slightly different ways, depending on the version of the Bible you are reading. Perhaps those translations that say that Christ *gives* the circumcision (circumcision *by* Christ) are the most straightforward. The New International Version, for example, puts it this way: "Your whole self ruled by the flesh was put off when *you were circumcised by Christ*" (italics mine). The Christ-given circumcision is dying to self, or the control your fleshly desires have over you, and allowing Christ to be master. The believer metaphorically lays himself on the surgical table and allows Christ to cut away the sinful self as a Jewish rabbi would have cut away the foreskin of a male child.

But other translations talk about Christ being the one who experiences circumcision. The New Century Version (NCV) is one of those. It says: "It was through Christ's circumcision, that is, *his death*, that you were made free from the power of your sinful self" (italics mine). As it is expressed in the NCV, we can interpret the circumcision to be an act of Christ *imputed* to us, rather than an act of Christ upon us. In other words, *His* death equals *our* circumcision.

Though these translations are different from each other, what is important is that we are no longer governed by our fleshly desires. Our self-mastery has been sacrificed. We are risen anew in Christ, and He is the master of our lives now.

The offer of the new circumcision is extended to every human being, whereas the old circumcision was only for boys, and only those born into the chosen nation. As F. F. Bruce pointed out, the old circumcision "being restricted to males, was . . . inappropriate for the new order in Christ."[1] The order of Christ has absolutely no prerequisites.

THE BAPTISM (COL. 2:12)

While water baptism was and still remains the most common way of outwardly demonstrating one's union with Christ, we must keep in mind that Paul was stressing that outward signs are not what is most important. This passage circles around this main point. Physical circumcision was not needed because spiritual circumcision was superior. The Colossians were not physically circumcised, but they had been physically baptized in water. Interestingly, baptism here does not represent death and resurrection. Circumcision is the representation of death, because through spiritual circumcision "your whole self ruled by the flesh was put off" (v. 11). Baptism represents *burial* and resurrection. The old self has been put to death and buried as proof of that fact. Immersion in water equals burial, and rising up out of the water equals resurrection. That's a lot of technicalities, and does it really matter? The important takeaway is that what happens in the heart and mind of a believer matters. Death to self and new life in Christ are what give us our new identity.

THE RESURRECTION (COL. 2:13)

Not only have we been given new life, but we have been made alive with Christ. We are united with Him. He is the source of life and we couldn't be alive—*truly* alive, in the way God intended—without Him.

I suppose no illustration for this concept is adequate, but I am reminded of a friend of mine who recently gave her kidney to the husband of a mutual friend. Once he was self-contained, but then he became sick. Now he is alive because of my friend's gift. I think of the strange connection my friend and this man now share. Just as his life depends on her organ, our lives depend on the life, wholeness, and resurrection of our Savior. We are not self-contained. No, we are in a far better situation! The New Revised Standard Version says, "God made you alive together with him."

In our sinful state we were at odds with Christ. Romans 5:10 says that we were enemies of God. That's strong language and it gives us a real understanding of how distant we were from Him. Having died to self, however, we chose to be resurrected and made alive together with Christ. We are now united with Him and can't live in the way of the "old man." It just doesn't make sense anymore.

REFLECTION QUESTIONS

1. Have you made a willful, personal decision to follow Christ, or are you just doing what your parents did? Would you say that you made yourself available to be circumcised in Christ?

2. What are your personal fleshly desires? Do they ever creep up again? How do you, or how should you handle them?

3. What does it mean for you to be alive together with Christ?

11

THE POWER OF THE CROSS

COLOSSIANS 2:14–15

When apartheid was dismantled in South Africa, the country boldly employed restorative justice in the form of the Truth and Reconciliation Commission. When the Commission held court, those who had perpetrated violence against people of color would confess their crimes. In the same trial, the victims or surviving members of families whose loved ones had been murdered would tell of the oppression, grief, and loss they had endured, right there in the presence of those who had caused their misery. Once the guilty had confessed and shown shame, and those impacted had spoken their piece, the Commission had the power to pardon the offender. It was an extraordinary thing that mimicked what God has done for us.

It is hard to imagine, but it is likely that many of the white men and women of South Africa genuinely believed that the extreme segregation of apartheid was just the natural order of things. Most of us consider ourselves to be good people doing generally acceptable things. We are unaware of our own shame before God. It's like going to a hotel and assuming the linens and carpets are pristine, until someone does the black light test. All kinds of things show up.

THE DEBT (COL. 2:14)

Our truth is that we have all sinned. Even some of the things we believe to be acceptable may be deplorable in God's eyes, as was the case with apartheid. The reconciliation of sinful humanity to our holy God is called the atonement. It was achieved at the cross and becomes activated in the life of any individual when he or she becomes truly remorseful for sin and embraces the sacrifice of Christ. You can find a number of metaphors in the New Testament that explain the atonement in varied ways, which is probably why theologians debate different "atonement theories."

The metaphor used in these verses is one of legal indebtedness. That is to say, the law of God has been broken by all people and all people owe a debt to God because of it.

F. F. Bruce stressed the fact that Jews and Gentiles alike had this legal debt:

> Paul insisted that Jews, who had received the divine law by revelation, and pagans, who had not received it—not in the same form, at least—were alike morally bankrupt before God and equally in need of his pardoning grace. Jews had disobeyed his will in the form in which they knew it (the law); pagans had disobeyed it in the form in which they knew it (the inner voice of conscience). But, like the creditor in the parable faced with his two debtors, "when they had nothing to pay, he frankly forgave them both (Luke 7:42)."[1]

All of us initially approach God as moral and spiritual paupers, with nothing to offer as payment for our vast debt. He cancels our debt not because He decided to let the matter go, but because the price was paid on our behalf. As Martin Luther said, "He does not give grace so freely that He has demanded no satisfaction, but rather He has given Christ as the one who makes the satisfaction for us."[2] Our identity is that of people who are so valued that the price for our debt would be paid by God's only Son. Without reservation. Because, as Berkhof said, God the Father loves us with "love which stops for nothing."[3]

THE TRIUMPH (COL. 2:15)

In ancient days, when the Roman army made a conquest it would demonstrate its glory upon returning home by marching through the city, displaying the valuables that were taken from the conquered people. Prisoners of war were shackled and would either trail behind or precede the procession in abject humiliation. The prisoners were made into a "public spectacle." The Colossians would have been familiar with this practice, so Paul used it as an illustration here.

Jesus has made a "public spectacle" of the "powers [rulers] and authorities." They were humiliated by the great work of Jesus on the cross. But who exactly were these powers and authorities, and in what way were they defeated?

The first power were those people who physically persecuted and killed Jesus—the Jewish and Roman authorities. They thought they had the last word. They thought they had eliminated an enemy. Oh, how wrong they were! They had neither stopped Jesus nor His message. The cross did not make a fool of Christ. Rather it exposed their own foolishness, their own lack of power. Their deeds against Christ were temporal while the voluntary sacrifice of Christ was cosmic and eternal. Perhaps as Paul wrote about Christ's triumph in this verse, he was thinking not only about the cross, but also of the empty tomb that completes the story.

In addition, the Roman and Jewish authorities that wielded "power" were put in check because the classism and racism that they vigilantly maintained were replaced at the cross. Christ created a new order in which all people are equal, regardless of race, gender, economic status, and so on. Those who had been devalued were now esteemed in a way that they could never have imagined, because God's only Son was not spared in order to save them.

Today, many people continue to be persecuted and marginalized, devalued by the temporary powers of the world. Such abuse has never ceased. But believers know that this is the curse of this shadowy life; it is not our identity in the eternal sense. Much more important than any earthly status or gain is the fact that we are the children of the King of the Universe, equalized and set free because of Calvary. This equality that is already a reality in God's eyes will be fleshed out in every way when Christ returns. But even before that great day, even on *this very day*, His church is to operate by this principle. The church is meant to boldly stare down a society that thrives on hierarchy and marginalization, proving that real love and equality are possible when the Master is in charge.

Finally, the cross disarmed and disgraced the spiritual authorities who desire to keep us in the bondage of sin. Satan lost God's favor and has made it his main business to guarantee that humans lose it, too. Our demise is his delight. But the Evil One and his minions were thoroughly defeated at the cross. All who wish to be in a holy relationship with God are able. We may shed the shackles of sin and be united with our Father because of the cross.

F. F. Bruce wrote: "The very instrument of disgrace and death by which the hostile forces thought they had him in their grasp and had conquered him forever was turned by him into the instrument of their defeat and disablement."[4]

Now the enemies of the Lord have become the public spectacle. As Bruce so eloquently stated, "The shameful tree has become the victor's triumphal chariot, before which his captives are driven in humiliating procession."[5]

REFLECTION QUESTIONS

1. When was the first time (in your memory) that you felt genuine shame for your sinful state? How did you approach God at that time?

2. Have you ever paid off a debt, a loan, a credit card, or something of the kind—or been forgiven of a debt? What did that feel like?

3. Take a moment and remember a personal deed that has brought you shame at some point. Visualize Christ removing the guilt and the shame. First, He forgives you because you are indeed guilty. Then He removes the heavy

burden of the shame that came with it. Can you picture that in your head somehow? Perhaps even draw a picture that represents that.

4. List the three types of powers/rulers and authorities who were defeated at the cross. How does that relate specifically to your life?

5. Have you ever suffered prejudice against yourself, and/or have you ever inflicted it upon another person (on the basis of race, gender, age, or anything else)? Why is it completely inappropriate for a Christian to engage in deeds or attitudes of prejudice? How can a Christian who is the victim of prejudice ensure that it doesn't impact his or her identity?

12

THE SHADOWS THAT WERE

COLOSSIANS 2:16–19

Imagine that you are interested in purchasing a new home, so you go online and you look at pictures of houses. With each house you can see pictures of the front yard, the backyard, and all the rooms inside. You settle on a home that looks just right to you. You are very impressed with its appearance. You contact a real estate agent and you purchase the house. You show all your friends the pictures online, and they comment on what a fine house you've bought. But you've never been to the actual house and neither have your friends. For all you know, the wood may be full of termites. The foundation may be sinking. You haven't seen the real thing; you've only seen an image of it. You and your friends draw conclusions about the worthiness of the home not because of what it is, but because of what it presents itself to be.

Similarly, imagine judging a person based a set of rules and rituals. It is easy to see whether or not a person is obedient to those accepted practices, but that method falls far short of learning who a person really is—whether or not her "house" is solidly built. The Colossians were being judged by what could be viewed from the outside and Paul directed them not to let themselves be defined in that way, as we will discover together in this study.

NOT RITUALS (COL. 2:16–17)

Eating the right food or following the spiritual customs says nothing of the condition of one's "house." Having said that, it should be made clear that these customs weren't silly. Paul referred to dietary regulations and religious celebrations as being "a shadow of the things that were to come" (v. 17). For generations before the coming of Christ these practices pointed to God's great plan, which was now fulfilled in Jesus Christ.

According to F. F. Bruce, "Many Jews looked on their festivals and sacred seasons as adumbrations [foreshadowings] of the messianic age."[1] So these special days and the dietary regulations that were sometimes an element of those observances were dripping with meaning (but not all dietary restrictions were associated with special days).

The New International Version has a helpful heading above 2:16 and the text following: "Freedom from Human Rules." It should be understood that this passage does not speak against the practice of fasting or abstaining or the practice of marking specific holy days. Rather, the conversation is about the human laws that had built up concerning these issues, and the fact that some people would judge the credibility of another person's faith on how well they followed these human laws.

But once the Messiah had indeed come, was there any point in sticking to the customs that *foretold* of His coming? Some of the earliest Christians may have thought they should observe these customs because their symbolism did not disappear with the coming of the Messiah. The celebrations not only addressed His coming, they also had identified the Jews as God's elected people. The new Christians understood that status now belonged to them; did they need to observe Jewish holy days to signify that fact?

Paul argued that the celebrations were no longer important. The foretelling of a Messiah was irrelevant, and the mark of distinction through festivals was unnecessary — status as part of God's chosen people was now announced through baptism and demonstrated through consistent holy living.

Additionally, it seems that Paul was concerned that the Colossians were approaching festivals in a syncretistic way.

That is to say, they were combining the pagan customs with the celebrations that had always been dedicated to Yahweh alone. Verses 18 and 20 are strongly connected to verses 16 and 17. In those verses Paul wrote about their inclusion of angel worship, visions, and worship of universal elements. Those who had come from a pagan background were fusing paganism with Christian faith. While festivals weren't forbidden in the new faith, if done, they had to be done to the glory of the one true God.

On the other hand, it could be the case that these dietary restrictions and religious celebrations were *forced* on the new Christians in Colossae by Judaizers, who insisted that all the ancient practices, in their distinctly Jewish way, be maintained by new believers in Christ. The Judaizers would not have seen Christianity as a new faith, but as the continuation of Judaism. (That nuance is *still* an interesting debate!) Again, Paul wanted everyone to understand that they were free from the old practices that pointed to Christ because Christ had already come, and he disregarded any idea of proving oneself as part of God's family by obeying the ancient customs.

While Paul did not forbid anyone from observing fasts, religious festivals, or the Sabbath, if done in honor of the true God, he did not tolerate believers being judged by whether or not they did these things. All that these rituals pointed to was fulfilled in the new age. Christ sent the Holy

Spirit as a seal on our lives. No other identifier is necessary.[2] When others look at our lives they should be able to discern that we are different. Rituals and limitations aren't what make us different. The love that pours through us, by the power of the Holy Spirit, is what makes us different. The pure lives we live in every moment, not just on specified holy days, make us different.[3]

THE SHADOWS (COL. 2:17)

According to Plato, the world of intellect and knowledge was the true world and the things we see around us are only shadows of what is real. Paul might have been drawing on this familiar Greek philosophy when he referred to the established religious practices as being "a shadow of the things that were to come."[4]

In the story Plato told to explain his notion, human beings were shackled by their necks in an underground den, unable to see or understand anything but the shadows, so they believed the shadows to be complete reality. Judaizers or other confused teachers in Colossae believed things like religious festivals to be critical realities—they were shackled to them. They were unable to see that these things were merely vague images of what Christ brought in complete fulfillment. N. T. Wright observes:

Christ has inaugurated the 'age to come.' The regulations of Judaism were designed for the period when the people of God consisted of one racial, cultural and geographical unit, and are simply out of date now that this people is becoming a world-wide family. They were the 'shadows' that the approaching new age casts before it. Now that the reality is come, there is no point in clinging to the shadows. And the reality belongs to Christ.[5]

HUMILITY AND ANGELS (COL. 2:18)

Judgmentalism always involves pride. It says, "my way is better than your way." If you read through the New Testament, you would have no doubt in your mind that Christians are to hold each other accountable in the faith. We are to teach and admonish and lead and follow and support. But we are never given permission to pass judgment on one another.

Perhaps one of the ugliest forms of pride that always results in judgmentalism is false humility. C. S. Lewis said, "A man is never so proud as when striking an attitude of humility."[6] In this passage some Colossians were very proud of how humble they were. They were likely fasting and obeying the rituals Paul just mentioned, and they considered that humble behavior. Self-righteous Christians were both condemning others for not following the rules and congratulating themselves for their humble obedience.

The self-righteous ones included those who worshiped angels. This practice is an example of the syncretism that was plaguing the Colossians: the mix of pagan ideas with Jewish tradition. Jews didn't worship angels, but pagans did worship beings from other realms, which would have been "Christianized" into the worship of angels.

An angel is a messenger from God. While we may not worship them today, one doesn't need look too far to come across Christians who worship God's messengers. Pastors, musicians, and Christian authors who are God's messengers are often put on pedestals. In a Facebook conversation about leadership, my friend Kevin aptly noted that "in some parts of the world in particular, the automatic, unquestioning glorification of leadership is bordering on idolatry." This often leads to devastation, or at least disappointment, because eventually every human's failings will come to the surface. We all know that God is "the only proper object of religious worship."[7] But sometimes we are worshiping something else without even realizing it. Louie Giglio says:

> So how do you know where and what you worship? It's easy. You simply follow the trail of your time, your affection, your energy, your money, and your loyalty. At the end of that trail you'll find a throne;

and whatever, or whomever, is on that throne is what's of highest value to you. On that throne is what you worship.[8]

The only one who should be on that throne is the Triune God.

DISCONNECTED (COL. 2:18–19)

The very things that people thought made them extra-spiritual were the products of unspiritual minds—minds focused on self rather than on Christ. No wonder verse 19 says that these people had lost connection with the head, which is Christ! The misguided, judgmental Christians claimed to see visions of angels as they worshiped them.

In the New Revised Standard Version, verse 18 reads this way: "Do not let anyone disqualify you, insisting on self-abasement and worship of angels, dwelling on visions, puffed up without cause by a human way of thinking." These ignorant people groveled before the angels that they imagined they were seeing, and they were foolishly proud of their visions.

Like many children, my friends and I used to play "Bloody Mary" at slumber parties when I was a child. One or two daring souls would go into the bathroom, turn out the lights, and recite "Bloody Mary, Bloody Mary" over and over. Eventually the girls in the bathroom were always certain they had actually seen the ghost of Mary, Queen of Scots, covered in blood, in the mirror (though at the time we didn't realize that was who we were calling upon). A fervent, earnest mind can be fooled when led by a silly notion.

The Christians Paul was criticizing had become disconnected from Christ. Some people are so wrapped up in their own minds, their own ideas, their own brilliant philosophies that they lose connection with what is true. Or, better said, they lose connection with who is Truth.

Look around you and see how many people think they can cobble together their own truth. Many people even draw from varied sources to invent their own brand of "Christianity." Jesus Christ made it clear and easy: "I am the way and the truth and the life. No one comes to the Father except through me" (John 14:6).

Adding to or deleting from the gospel is nothing but foolishness. We don't get to make up what is true—frankly, we should be relieved to know that. There is a real truth and it doesn't come from our frail, fallible minds. I would never stake my present joy and eternal future on a belief system I had developed out of my own reasoning. Tragically, many people seem to do that. Even some of the people sitting in our worship services on Sunday morning pick and choose what they like theologically, as if the gospel were a grand buffet.

Do you want to know what is true? God the Son brought truth in the flesh when He descended to earth as one of us. And God the Holy Spirit continues to help us understand truth through Scripture and prayer and meditative thought and the wisdom of fellow believers. It is nothing short of ridiculous to reject truth from the initiator of all things in favor of building our own version of truth in our finite minds.

Only those who remain connected to the Head will grow and flourish. Those who self-design their faith based on their limited understanding have chosen their own heads over The Head—and in the process, they lose connection with the rest of the body of Christ. Their spiritual survival is at stake.

REFLECTION QUESTIONS

1. Can you think of any customs or rituals at your church or in the church as a whole that you think are still full of meaning?

2. Reflect on the following statement: "Christ has sent the Holy Spirit as a seal on our lives. No other identifier is necessary." Do you agree or disagree? Why?

3. Is your faith based purely on what is scriptural and understood by the church? Have you self-designed your faith in any way to make it easier?

4. Is anything or anyone besides God sitting on your heart's throne today?

13

HUMAN COMMANDS

COLOSSIANS 2:20–23

I'm always shocked to learn about things people once thought should be off-limits for Christians. Not long ago, I was watching a television series based on the Anne of Green Gables books, which is set in the late nineteenth century. One of the characters—a little girl—said that her mother told her that all manner of "playacting" was evil. In other words, children were permitted to play, but they weren't allowed to *pretend*. Now, it seems to me that unless you're engaging in a sport, playing without pretending to be someone else— a hero or a "bad guy," a crotchety old woman, a teacher, or whatever—is nearly impossible. What a tremendous restriction that would place on the imagination of a child! And for what reason? How could playacting be harmful?

I don't know whether nineteenth-century Christians actually believed that playacting was evil, but when I consider other religious regulations I've heard, the idea doesn't seem far-fetched. Throughout time, eager proponents of just about any faith have placed layers of restrictions on people. Within Christianity, churches in the Holiness Movement—such as mine—may be particularly culpable. The conviction that one needs to lead a holy life seems to lend itself to the idea that holiness can be regulated.

Why does faith often decompose into just a set of rules? Maybe it is easier to follow a list of dos and don'ts than it is to develop a real relationship with Christ. Maybe living by "yes" and "no" is easier than living by the *spirit* of the law. Or maybe it has something to do with the biblical narrative.

FREEDOM IN THE NEW IDENTITY (COL. 2:20–22)

Judaism really crystalized as a faith when Moses received the Ten Commandments—a list of rules. The Torah actually has 613 laws of Moses, though the original ten are the monumental laws that set the tone for all other instruction. Beyond that, religious leaders had constructed the Mishnah, which was "an oral tradition of commentary on the Mosaic law that introduced additional, man-made rules that 'built a fence' around the Mosaic law so people wouldn't even come close to breaking God's commandments."[1]

As the Christians in Colossae struggled to understand their new identity as people of a traditionally Jewish God, they felt compelled (or were pressured) to assume the ancient Jewish laws and customs. From Paul's comment that the rules were about things that "perish with use," we get the impression that he was mostly referring to dietary restrictions, which had much to do with the religious celebrations mentioned earlier, and nothing to do with salvation through Christ.

The Colossians didn't fully understand that restrictive practices had been replaced by the reality of Christ and that Jewish law had been a placeholder until Christ came to do His perfect salvation work. The law had been designed to help people live a life that would please and not offend God, but now through the sacrificial blood of Christ they were not offensive to God, just as they were.

Another one of Paul's letters puts it succinctly:

Before the coming of this faith, we were held in custody under the law, locked up until the faith that was to come would be revealed. So the law was our guardian until Christ came that we might be justified by faith. Now that this faith has come, we are no longer under a guardian. So in Christ Jesus you are all children of God through faith. (Gal. 3:23–26)

Of course, to be in Christ is not to throw all principles of spiritual living to the wind. The fact that this passage tells the Colossians—and us—not to be bound by the "don'ts" doesn't mean we have license to do whatever we want. It is our privilege to live lives that are pleasing to God through the power of the Holy Spirit. But this life does involve effort. It is more than sitting in a church service or praying on your couch, feeling holy. The New Testament is full of instruction about how to live a life that pleases God. (We will see some of this in Colossians 3.) Second Timothy 2:15 points out that God expects us to live intentionally holy lives rather than just sit back and enjoy our status as saved people:

> Do your best to present yourself to God as one approved, a worker who does not need to be ashamed and who correctly handles the word of truth.

As we read Colossians 2, we must remember that Paul was trying to help the Colossians understand that traditional restrictions were not required for salvation and were not evidence of a vital life in Christ. He is not condoning a libertine lifestyle, or even just a spiritually lazy lifestyle. His point was not that instruction for righteous living should be discarded, but that our salvation isn't contingent upon following the old rites, which had been constructed by humans in the first place.

IMPOTENT RULES (COL. 2:23)

Not only were the human-made rules no longer necessary, but they also weren't effective for really changing people. Rules aren't equipped to change the heart, and when the heart isn't convinced, obedience is a struggle.

Even today, people try to reduce the gospel to a set of rules. They believe you aren't proving yourself a good Christian if you don't succumb to whatever regulations they deem important.[2] But Christianity is about a relationship with Christ. Those who love Christ find that His guidelines for life—His "rules," if you will—have not been given to us to burden us.

As a child I attended a Christian elementary school. The staff was limited, and the classroom teachers had to take turns monitoring us at recess. Many of us feared the days that fifth-grade teacher Mrs. Woodward had recess duty. She didn't smile, and she had a whistle she blew quite often to arrest any wayward behavior. She was stricter and more mean-faced than the other teachers. When it was time for me to enter fifth grade, I was terrified to discover I'd been assigned to Mrs. Woodward's class. But as I got to know her, I grew to adore her. She was smart and kind and inspirational.

One day Mrs. Woodward said something that changed my life forever. She looked at the class and said, "All of you know how to read. Therefore, all of you are old enough to read your Bible every day." I loved and respected Mrs. Woodward, and I took to heart what she said. I didn't receive her admonishment as another rule that had to be followed. I accepted it as wise advice—a guideline that would help me. I became a Bible-reader at a fairly tender age because of her.

When I saw Mrs. Woodward as no one but a dispenser of laws, I kept my distance. But once I was in a relationship with her, I didn't resent her rules anymore because she was someone I trusted. I no longer saw her as someone trying to obstruct my fun. I understood that she was just concerned with the safety of everyone on the playground.

A set of rules will not turn a rebellious person into a submissive one. Rules don't curb the desire to push limits. Behavior is changed when a person believes in the rules or the rule-setter. Colossians 2:23 is about rules that are unimportant because they are ineffective: they don't restrain sensual indulgence. Sensual indulgence is restrained when a person's heart is won by Christ and the limits begin to make sense.

Why, you might ask, is it important to control fleshly desires at all if we are saved by grace, not by good behavior? Restraining indulgence is for the benefit of ourselves and others. It is the loving and wise thing to do. Imagine the fallout if a person gave in to every sexual desire, for example. Family is hurt. Partners are hurt. Unwilling victims may fall prey as the person acts upon his lust, and the list goes on. Eventually even the perpetrator is left with the internal pain his own destructive behavior has caused. On both a small scale and a large scale, sensual indulgence is steeped in selfishness, and no one wins in such a situation.

Instead, let us constantly reflect the kind of love that Christ demonstrated and also placed in our hearts. As people who are dead to this world but alive in Christ we should exhibit controlled behavior that comes from a loving heart, not a list of rules.

REFLECTION QUESTIONS

1. Have you seen Christians attempt to force nonbiblical rules on each other to prove their holiness? What did that look like?

2. Do you ever judge fellow Christians by standards you think are important but can't exactly be found in the Bible?

3. Why should we not interpret this passage in Colossians 2 as permission to live however we please?

4. In what way are God's "rules" for everyone's benefit, not our frustration?

14

THE THINGS ABOVE

COLOSSIANS 3:1–4

A little girl at my church recently told me that she was very bothered by the idea that Jesus was everywhere, because it meant He could see everything she was doing. She went on to tell me that her grandmother had explained that Jesus was in her heart and "that made me feel a lot better." In the literal mind of a little girl, having Jesus safely tucked away in her heart meant that He couldn't witness all her deeds and misdeeds!

We all use clumsy phrases to explain to our children where Jesus *is* because we don't completely understand it ourselves. When Jesus ascended to the Father, He sent the Holy Spirit to comfort and guide us. The Holy Spirit is ever present with us. But it is safe to assume that Jesus is with us, too. He said He would be with us even to the "end of the age" (Matt. 28:20). Factor in that the Holy Spirit, Jesus, and the Father are all one God, "undivided in essence,"[1] and it further boggles the mind.

Is it even possible to pin down the location of God? Perhaps physical placement is just a human attempt to understand who God is and what He does and how this universe operates. Truly He is metaphysical, and we cannot grasp that. At the same time, it is appropriate to think of the person of Jesus—second person of the Trinity—as someone very physical. He is God and man; it is His eternal identity.

WHERE CHRIST IS (COL. 3:1)

Colossians 3:1 says that Jesus is above, seated at the right hand of the Father. To some extent the physicality of that statement matters. Christ is seated in the heavenly realm, which, no matter where it may be located, is beyond this world and is different from this world at *least* in the fact that it is sinless and perfect. In this location "above," Christ reigns fully, unlike here on planet Earth. This heavenly realm is representative of the kingdom to which we now already belong because we are dead to the ways of this world. Our true citizenship is in a kingdom that is not what we currently experience here.

In another sense, the idea of a physical throne in a heavenly realm doesn't matter so much—the symbolism of it is what is important. The "right hand" figuratively expressed a position of honor. A description of Christ in a realm above seated at the right hand of God represents His majesty and deity. This language first appears in Psalm 110:1:

> The LORD says to my lord:
> "Sit at my right hand
> until I make your enemies
> a footstool for your feet."

At His trial before the Sanhedrin, Christ claimed these words as a descriptor of Himself (see Matt. 26:63–66). The people immediately understood that He was claiming to be Almighty God. The high priest cried blasphemy and ripped his garment, and others agreed that He was worthy of death for appropriating the words of the psalm. So, we can see that these words are powerful.

OUR POSITION (COL. 3:1, 3–4)

Christ's heavenly position at the right hand of the Father has direct bearing on those who are saved. We are meant to identify with Christ's post-resurrection life, because we have been raised with Him. The identity we had before salvation has been abandoned. More than abandoned, it has been put to death! Our new identity—our new life—is hidden in Him. We cannot consider our lives except in relation to His.

So, while we still live in this imperfect age before the second coming of Christ, we are citizens of the eternal kingdom. While our physical eyes cannot even perceive the presence of Christ, our spiritual eyes see Him on His throne, glorified, reigning as King of Kings. Someday the kingdom to which we belong will be as real as the grass in our own front yard or the chair you're now sitting in. We would do well to remind ourselves that what is coming is not a fantasy! It is the reality we eagerly anticipate.

What a strange and wonderful position we find ourselves in now. Our minds and hearts are filled with eternal realities. And yet, as we dwell in this present space, we find that Christ meets us here. He does not neglect us. Metaphorically speaking, His throne is not too lofty for us to ascend. Or perhaps it is better to say that we are not so debased that He will not descend to meet with us. He did it in a very tangible way two thousand years ago, and He does it today in a way that is not as obvious but just as real.

YOUR HEARTS AND MINDS (COL. 3:1–2)

Both our hearts (v. 1) and our minds (v. 2) are to be focused on things that are from above, not things of earth.

Because our lives are hidden in Christ and we are citizens of His eternal kingdom, it only makes sense that we pursue the values of that reality, not of this one. Our hearts—our emotional center—should long for what is good and holy. Our minds—the center of our thought and conscious decision—should be dedicated to what is good and holy.

As Salvation Army officers my husband and I are reassigned to new positions and locations every few years. To facilitate such a system, the Army owns the homes in which their officers live. Not only the home, but also the furniture, the pots and pans, almost everything.[2] My husband and I had assignments in Alexandria, Virginia for six years. That's a pretty long time for Salvation Army officers, and we allowed our roots to sink in. We loved our life there, and we loved our home. One of the things I enjoyed about our home was the colors of the walls. The previous officers had left the hallways white but painted each room a different color. (It sounds wilder than it was.) I thought it was beautiful and full of personality. I was very attached to that home.

After six years in Alexandria, we moved across the country to our next appointment and a new set of Army officers moved into the home we loved. A couple of weeks after our move we returned to Virginia to perform a wedding, so we decided to drive past our old house. When we did, the door was open and I, of course, rolled down my car window to peer inside the house as hard as I could.

I was devastated to see that the walls had been repainted. Shortly after that, our son who remained in Virginia went to the house for a Bible study. He confirmed that everything had been repainted—and then he was coldhearted enough to suggest that it was an improvement!

I was immensely fond of our new house in Seattle, but I was still attached to the home we had left. Letting go of it was a painful process for me. Even though my body was three thousand miles away, my heart was attached to our old teal bedroom, yellow kitchen and red powder room, our great square dining room table, and some of the best neighbors we'd had ever had. Eventually I had to place all of that in a file in my mind marked "Happy Memories" and fully engage myself in my exciting new ministry and life.

Old loves are not easily discarded. Even when something better comes along, we can find ourselves longing for what was familiar and comfortable. If that weren't the case, Paul wouldn't have to remind his readers to focus on the things above rather than the things of this world. Though we've left the "old man" for dead and been resurrected in Christ, we sometimes try to do a little gravedigging, scooping up old habits and ungodly choices we used to find pleasure in. Returning to sinful behaviors is senseless, but we do lapse so easily into it, don't we? We can be like Lot's wife—we cannot imagine that there's something better ahead and we turn longingly to what was.

I have the privilege of having a fairly new Christian in my life right now. I'm close to her, and I see her just about every day. Before she received salvation and began a relationship with Christ, she was a pleasant person, easy to be around. But since she has come to know Christ as Savior, I have watched her blossom into a fruitful, fragrant Christian—a shining, beautiful light for Christ. She told me that her previous desire to be kind to others was rooted in her need to feel like a good person for her own sake, but now she just wants to "be like the Perfect One."

I have watched the renewing of her mind (see Rom. 12:2), and that mind is now set on things above. In her I see what it is to die to self and be risen in Christ, with new life hidden in Him. And if you were to ask her, she would tell you that it is much better than clinging to the old way, with one's heart and mind set on things of this earth.

REFLECTION QUESTIONS

1. Do you envision Christ as being in heaven sitting on a throne, or in the room with you, or some sort of combination of both (or something else altogether)?

2. Take a moment to consider Christ in a new light. If you usually think of Him as Divine Lord, take a moment to consider His physicality. If you think of Him as a man,

imagine Him now on His universal throne. Perhaps draw a picture that demonstrates your thoughts.

3. What type of worldly things interest you? Are any of these things inappropriate for Christians?

4. Are there old behaviors you cast off when you got saved? Are there habits that you need to cast off now? How can you set your heart and mind on things that are from above?

15

THE OLD IDENTITY
COLOSSIANS 3:5–8

My husband and I once had two little sisters in our congregation who were rather neglected at home. They were sweet children, but quite dirty and scraggly. A few of us women decided we'd take them shopping for new Easter dresses and shoes one year. When all was purchased, I was so excited to see them on Easter morning! They did indeed show up in their beautiful new dresses and shoes, but they themselves were as dirty as ever—hair greasy and unbrushed, faces smudged with breakfast, hands still stained from outdoor play. There was a disconnect between the elegant clothing and the disheveled little children who wore the clothing. Similarly, when we come to Christ it is incongruous for us to live the way we once did. The soiled way of the world is part of our old identity, completely unsuitable for a follower of Jesus.

PUTTING EARTHLY WAYS TO DEATH (COL. 3:5)

The preceding verses (3:1–2) insist that those who have been raised with Christ must focus on "things above." Later verses spell out what some of these things from above are, but first, in verses 5–8 we have a list of their opposites. These things are *earthly*. Paul continually contrasted the old life with the new, saved life: we move from death to life, from regulated to free, from earthly-minded to heavenly-minded (concerned about the things of the kingdom of God). When a person enters into relationship with Christ, his salvation means that his life makes a 180-degree turn. These contrasts are helpful so that we can understand how completely our lives should change.

One might protest that one wasn't such a horrible person before salvation. But really, the dramatic change is in the heart and mind. A nice guy who pays his taxes and treats his friends and family well but doesn't have a relationship with Jesus is likely to be unaware of or unconcerned about some of the things listed in verses 5 and 8. Here, the Christian is told that these things cannot be tolerated in a holy life. The heart must change.

Of course, getting saved doesn't suddenly vanquish every ungodly thought and desire. Paul writes about this subject because we are to *actively, consciously* put these things to death. Completely killing them off can be done only through the power of the Holy Spirit, and I think it is fair to say that Paul assumes this, though he doesn't mention it.

As mentioned in study 5, I believe it is possible to live in victory over sin. There is never a time when we, who are filled with the Holy Spirit, are powerless against temptation. However, it is a very common Christian experience to live with "Whac-a-Mole sins." Let me explain: Whac-a-Mole is a fun game to play at an arcade. The player has a soft hammer with which to pound "moles" as they pop up out of holes. But after the mole has been whacked, it pops up again. It multiplies, in fact, and pops up all over the large game board. It may let up a bit, but then it will come back full force!

Certain sins seem to have that Whac-a-Mole tenacity. That old temptation for that favorite sin seems unconquerable. You think you've got it handled, but it pops up again. It becomes increasingly insistent on making its appearance. There is an ultimate way to stop the moles from popping up in the arcade game: unplug the machine and walk away! Pet sins will finally be conquered when they receive no more power, when they are ignored rather than fed.

A Christian who wants victory can't dwell in places where her temptations are powered. She must deliberately avoid certain situations and maybe even certain people so nothing is fueling her temptation. In time, the temptation—depleted of power and left for dead—no longer has the strength to even show itself. This is all possible when the mind of the Christian is set on things from above, and no attention is given to anything else. If this were not possible, we would not be instructed to put the old ways to *death*.

THE FIRST LIST (COL. 3:5–6)

Two lists of sins that reflect earthliness—or the unsaved way of living—are given in this passage. According to Ralph Martin, the first list "has chiefly sexual sins in its sight."[1] In the ESV they are listed as "sexual immorality, impurity, passion, [and] evil desire." Certainly sexual desire is one of the greater struggles that Christians face. It doesn't help that our society does all it can to tantalize!

Though God created us as sexual beings, He intended us to approach that part of ourselves in a sacred, holy way and to treat others with the same dignity. We are well aware that it is inappropriate to make unwanted advances or comments to someone. But if we view others as precious and beloved by God, we understand that even entertaining private salacious fantasies about someone is a mistreatment of that person from God's viewpoint.

The other word in the first list is *covetousness* (ESV; NIV and NRSV both use *greed*). This term could carry a sexual meaning, too. One of the things the Israelites had been instructed not to covet was another man's wife (see Ex. 20:17). But any time a person looks at something someone else has and desperately wants it, she is coveting. It is idolatry to covet because her mind becomes fixated on the object of her desire rather than on God and the things from above. Whatever inches God off the throne of our hearts is an idol to us.

These lecherous sins are enough to incite the wrath of God. There is mercy for those who ask for forgiveness. But for those who cling to sin, unhappy repercussions await, both in this life and the next.

Perhaps the sins on this first list are especially egregious because they destroy the dignity of human beings. They insult the image of God in individual people. To approach others as merely vehicles for one's own sexual satisfaction is debasing and degrading. In addition, to place any object of one's desire ("covetousness, which is idolatry") above God Himself is preposterous. He is the worthy one. He is the source of love and mercy and in Him we find all we need. Our lives are to be resurrected with Him and hidden in Him. It is the gravest of errors to put anything or anyone else on the throne of one's heart.

THE SECOND LIST (COL. 3:8)

Martin said that the sins in the second list "all have to do with the human power of speech."[2] Though some scholars interpret *wrath* (ESV; translated *rage* in the NIV) as more of an emotion, according to Martin and others we can understand both anger and wrath to mean fits of temper that lead to verbal outbursts. Either way, what comes out of the mouth begins as a swell of rage in the heart first. The more a heart is reformed by the Holy Spirit, the less frequently anger rises up in it. The goal is not to feel anger in the first place (except in extreme and appropriate circumstances). The more we view others through the eyes of Christ, with godly compassion and patience, the less they irritate us.

Malice also has to do with the things that come out of a person's mouth. Malicious speech is meant to hurt another person. A parent who addresses his teenager's failings in an attempt to develop her is not being malicious. But a peer who highlights those failings in order to hurt and embarrass the teen is. And closely related to malice is slander, which has the intent of destroying a person's reputation. Gossip is peppered with slander. It puts the person talked about in a bad light; it changes the way people feel about that person.

The last in this second list is "obscene talk" (ESV). This is not only foul language and ungodly chatter, but also talk that personally insults or just generally offends other people. Obscene talk has become rampant in many Christian circles and those who are offended by it are often made to feel as though they just aren't "keeping it real." Words you wouldn't let your children say, and coarse talk in general, flows from the mouths of "hip" church leaders. It is hard to see how this reflects a loving, generous, kind heart. The speech itself is offensive, and the offense is compounded by a judgmental attitude towards those who appear startled when they hear it.

The way we speak is one of the key ways in which we distinguish ourselves from the world. In high school, other kids said to my sons: "You never swear. Why is that?" Everyone speaks, and how each person speaks is noticed and known. It identifies us. We want to be known as bringers of peace, people of love and light. Crass humor, foul language, vulgar stories, hurtful sarcasm—these things don't belong.

In Matthew 12:34, Jesus said: "The mouth speaks the things that are in the heart" (NCV). As people who have put the "old man" to death, our reformed hearts should be filled with love. When the sin of a loose tongue keeps popping up Whac-a-Mole style, the line that powers it has to be cut. Situations that promote inappropriate speech need to be avoided. The habit of focusing on people's shortcomings or things that are negative needs to be replaced with finding the good in others.

Both lists of earthly behavior are focused on how we treat other people. It is imperative to remember that every human being on earth was created in the image of God and, as such, is endowed with great dignity. Though all have sinned and greatly marred the image of God within themselves, our responsibility is to treat all persons as they were created: worthy of love and respect.

REFLECTION QUESTIONS

1. Do you have any Whac-a-Mole sins? What are they? What is your understanding of how to conquer them?

2. Read the sins in Paul's list in verse 5 and explain them in your own words. Do you struggle with any of these things?

3. Why do these particular sins incite God's wrath?

4. List the sins in Paul's list in verse 8 and explain them in your own words. Do you struggle with any of these things?

5. What are your beliefs about cursing, coarse language, sarcasm, and so on, in the life of a Christian?

16

THE NEW IDENTITY

COLOSSIANS 3:9–11

Of our four sons, three are men and one is a preteen. My husband and I are now witnessing in our fourth son what we've seen with each of the older ones. Just weeks after his shoes have been replaced, they start cramping his feet. New pants can't keep up with his sprouting legs. He reports that he is unbearably hungry about every hour. And now, peach fuzz. I look at his school pictures lined up on our hallway wall and realize that this boy doesn't exist anymore. An emerging man, all limbs and cracking voice, has taken his place. The old person is being sloughed off. In a figurative but even more powerful way, the same is true with those who claim new identity in Christ.

OFF WITH THE OLD SELF (COL. 3:9)

In verse 5 Paul used the potent image of putting to death the old ways, the earthly ways. Here he used the image of taking something off and putting something on. This may be likened to taking off old, tattered, odorous garments and replacing them with something new and beautiful. Or perhaps it is closer to what F. F. Bruce wrote:

You see, he goes on, you have stripped off the "old man" that you used to be, together with the practices in which he loved to indulge. This was emphasized in Col. 2:11–22, where their baptism was said to be, in effect, not the removal of an insignificant scrap of bodily tissue, as the old circumcision was, but the stripping off of the whole "body of flesh"—the renunciation of the sinful nature in its entirety.[1]

The former self is to be completely gone—stripped off, crucified. Any way you look at it, he's gone.

With the old impulses and lifestyle abandoned, the Christian has no business lying. In the last study we discussed how our speech is one of the surest ways that people can identify believers as being separate from the world. A completely truthful person is a rare find. If we exhibit that level of integrity, we stand out as people of God. Integrity is also an important part of respecting and loving others. No one feels well treated when lied to, even when the lie is told in an effort to protect one's feelings.

ON WITH THE NEW SELF (COL. 3:10)

Colossians 2:6 is the book's thesis, summing up the heart of the letter. And if that verse is the summary, then 3:10 is the apex of the book. Heretofore, the theology has been presented, the old lifestyle has been declaimed, and now Paul succinctly presents this take-home message: You have accepted a new identity, and the new you is growing more and more like Christ every day.

Knowledge is an important piece of this growth because the more we know Christ, the more we can emulate Him. We are renewed people, people of the new order and not of the old. But our new selves still have room to grow as our understanding of Christ becomes progressively clearer. Even the most experienced, most dedicated saint can continue to become more like Christ as he learns more about Him.

So, we are to treat each other well, not as we did when living in our old identity. The "old man" is dead. He has been shed like a snake's outer layer of unwanted skin. What is left is a new person with a dignified identity who should be extending dignity to others as well.

CHASING EQUALITY (COL. 3:11)

I cannot overstate God's concern for the way we treat other people, especially fellow Christians. In this passage Paul's discussion of our new identity is bound to how we treat each other. Carrying that thought forward, he makes it clear that all of God's people are equal. None is better than the other.

In modern Western society, hierarchy exists. The structure isn't made formal by our governmental systems, and most people would argue that it isn't even morally right, but it's there. The wealthy are valued above the poor. The educated are considered a cut above those who aren't. The physically attractive are assigned more worth than the plain. It was similar in the ancient world, but in their day, hierarchy was the framework of society. To the ancient mind, this was the way the world functioned; nothing was amiss about it. In verse 11, Paul listed the social-ethnic groups that the Colossians knew well.

- Greeks (*Gentiles* in the NIV): world-conquerors, sophisticates, a privileged society (generally speaking)
- Jews: cultic, ultra-conservative, non-cosmopolitan
- Circumcised: full members of the Jewish faith
- Uncircumcised: outside of the Jewish faith (and perhaps unqualified for the new Christian faith)

- Barbarians: those who couldn't speak Greek, therefore the simpletons of the world
- Scythians: the lowest kind of barbarians, many of whom were slaves, barely better than wild animals
- Slaves: property of another person, having no human value in themselves
- Free: not someone else's property

As new people in Christ, the Colossians were part of a new kingdom. This kingdom had none of the class, ethnic, or racial divisions that Colossians saw as normal. (There was no longer any tolerance for hierarchy in terms of gender, either. See Gal. 3:28.) Paul never tried to erase cultural differences. He allowed for Jewish Christians to keep their observances and for Greeks to remain uncircumcised. The point of God's kingdom is not to homogenize everyone, but for us to embrace each other as we are. God is creative and has made us unlike one another in many ways. That is to be celebrated. What Paul did work to erase was superiority and inferiority. Christ died for all; to see one person as more worthy than another is offensive to God.

The congregation my husband and I pastor has roughly 160 regular attenders. It is a delightful mix of all sorts of people: men, women, and children in every age group; every major racial group; college professors and students, business professionals, concrete layers, housecleaners; singles and marrieds; people with ample homes and people who have struggled with homelessness. If you asked every person what his or her native language was, you would get over a dozen different answers. It is a genuine slice of the kingdom.

But even so, we find multitudes of reasons why people might assess and exclude one another. At our church, we have a significant number of people who are either in substance abuse rehabilitation or have graduated from "rehab." Over the past few years the segment of the congregation who hasn't struggled with addiction has been learning how to embrace those who have. We have witnessed the development of some lovely friendships (and even one marriage!). Not everyone has learned how to bridge the gap, of course—and that goes both ways. Some "normies" (a word coined by the recovery community, not by me) prefer to stay in their comfort zone. But likewise, some of those from the recovery community are not open to the hand of friendship extended by the normies because they feel the normies wouldn't be able to understand their lives. Neither group gets a pass for shutting other people out.

ELIMINATING DIVISIONS (COL. 3:11)

Verse 11 tells us that "Christ is all, and is in all." He is everything; He is the supreme one; He is all that matters.

And He dwells within all the people who are found in His church, which means He dwells in all the types of people who are on this planet. This hearkens back to the lofty praise language of chapter 1:

Christ is all:

The Son is the image of the invisible God, the first-born over all creation. For in him all things were created: things in heaven and on earth, visible and invisible, whether thrones or powers or rulers or authorities; all things have been created through him and for him. (1:15–16)

Christ is in all:

He is before all things, and in him all things hold together. And he is the head of the body, the church; he is the beginning and the firstborn from among the dead, so that in everything he might have the supremacy. (1:17–18)

Christ who is the head of the body is also the creator of humankind—*all* humankind. He does not tolerate a system that allows for one person to be seen as better than another. He does not tolerate a system where any person is less loved or less accepted than another. Let us be ever mindful, because tolerance isn't just about niceties. A world without division is the structure of the kingdom of God. If we are ranking and rating and judging and excluding, we are not living a kingdom lifestyle. We are not living as new selves were intended to live.

REFLECTION QUESTIONS

1. If you were to describe what it is like to get rid of the old self and take on the new self, what imagery would you use?

2. What is the "take-home message" for this study? Do you agree, or have you found another message you consider to be the main thrust? What other important points from Colossians stand out to you so far?

3. If the list of people groups in verse 11 were being written today, what kind of groups do you think would be listed? Who does your society look down upon, and who does it regard as superior?

4. Where do your prejudices lie? Do you think of yourself as "better than" specific people or groups?

17

BEING GOD'S CHOSEN PEOPLE

COLOSSIANS 3:12

When I was in college, one of our choirs was chosen to represent the United States at a worldwide festival, based on the long-standing reputation of the choir. But the choir's personnel changed every year. Though the choir had been chosen, its members had not been selected yet. Anyone in the whole university could audition. The same opportunity is available in the kingdom of God. Of course, we don't have to audition (thank God!), and even better, membership is a free gift—one we couldn't earn even if we did try. What does it mean to be a part of that kingdom? We'll unpack that as we dive into this passage.

WHO ARE GOD'S CHOSEN?

Israel was originally God's chosen group of people. Most everyone who belonged to that group was born into it,[1] and the males demonstrated their special status as the chosen through the physical act of circumcision. In the new order through Jesus, Christians became God's chosen people. You can't be born into Christianity, and no physical act gains you admission. But anyone can self-elect to be a Christian by deciding to follow Christ.

Therefore, we must view the terminology of verse 12 keeping the thrust of the passage in mind. To take the phrase "God's chosen people" from this sentence and use it as evidence for the doctrine of election would be inappropriate.[2] It doesn't speak about God inviting some in and leaving others out. Quite the contrary: the verse is about inclusiveness. The point made in 3:11 that all are who are in the new kingdom (i.e., all who have been saved by Christ and are part of His church) are equal, also implies that all people of the world are welcome to be part of that new kingdom. Verse 12, then, is about that fact that the church is now the chosen people group. As with the choir, the *group* has been chosen, and everyone has an opportunity to decide whether they want to be in the group or not.

WHAT DOES HOLINESS LOOK LIKE?

The Colossians were labeled "holy and dearly loved." The word "holy" can be theologically nuanced, as has been mentioned, so it also must be understood in light of its context. In this case, we understand it to mean "set apart." The Colossian Christians were not holy in the sense of having consistent victory over sin. Paul was actively instructing them how to live a godly lifestyle, so it was not something they had mastered. They were holy because they were part of that chosen group. They were different from the rest of the world because they had been washed in the blood of Jesus Christ.

Even as we grow in holiness, as we gain victory over the sins that beset us and become more Christlike, we already have a holy status because we have decided to be part of the chosen people. I have previously quoted F. F. Bruce as saying that ridding ourselves of our ungodly characteristics was truly "stripping off the 'whole body of flesh.'"[3] Because Paul instructed us to clothe ourselves with godly characteristics, perhaps it is not overreaching to say that these new clothes are like a new skin, replacing the flesh we've stripped off.

Think of an artist painting a fresco. He paints his water-colors directly into the wet plaster of a wall so that the paint doesn't just sit on top of the wall, it becomes part of it. In the same way, we Christians should don traits that become a veritable part of who we are, not something we put on and take off according to our mood.

Paul very clearly gave the Colossians (and us) a description of what that holiness in action looks like. His list of characteristics of our new selves contains everyday words, but they have weighty meaning:

- **Compassion:** We can find several instances in the Gospels where Jesus had compassion for people. In each of those instances, His compassion prompted Him to do something to relieve their plight—He taught, healed, or fed them, depending on the situation. Compassion is more than a feeling; it spurs us on to make adjustments and sacrifices in our own lives to address the needs of others.
- **Kindness:** The kindness of God when seen in Scripture is connected to His generosity and grace. God has been "kind" in offering us salvation when we deserved retribution. It is distressing how readily we mistreat one another when God has been so liberal with His grace. We must not be like the servant who had a great debt forgiven by his master but then turned around and imprisoned a fellow servant for a small debt he couldn't repay (see Matt. 18: 21–35). As kindness has been shown us, so we must show it to others.

- **Humility:** We exercise humility when we honor one another above ourselves (see Rom. 12:10). This attitude does not mean we have a poor opinion of ourselves. Christ was Lord of the universe, and yet He showed humility in coming to earth. His love was so expansive that He diminished His own situation for our sakes. He certainly didn't have low self-esteem! When we live humbly, we take care of our own needs, but not necessarily all of our desires. We take a backseat; we promote others.

- **Gentleness:** In 2018, a documentary about the life of Fred Rogers—*Won't You Be My Neighbor?*—was released. Viewers saw that Mr. Rogers' meek and tender manner wasn't just part of a television persona. The movie featured footage of him in conversation with some of his little fans. Whenever he encountered a child, he listened to every word that child had to say as though he or she were the most important person on earth. He never rushed them, and he had great respect for their thoughts and emotions. He treated them as people of value. He approached children gently and received them patiently. A gentle person is never forceful or pushy or impatient.

- **Patience:** Those who are patient extend two main things: time and grace. A patient parent understands that a child needs time to develop whatever skill or moral understanding the parent is looking for in her child. She also understands that grace is needed as the child makes repeated mistakes—or even repeated intentional sins. This kind of patience can and should be spread liberally between Christian brothers and sisters, and even to those outside the faith.

Each of these character traits requires valuing other people. We can easily say that we love others, but Paul was very specific about what that should look like. We aren't talking about nebulous generalities here. It is the hard stuff, the real stuff. We must evaluate whether we are showing this type of love to our family, our neighbors, members of the body of Christ, people with whom we work—everyone.

REFLECTION QUESTIONS

1. When was the last time you were moved by compassion to do something that involved an adjustment or sacrifice in your own life?

2. Can you remember a time when someone was kind enough to offer you grace when you needed it? How did it make you feel?

3. Is there any area in your life in which you are attempting to push yourself ahead of someone else? What would be your best, most humble move in the situation?

4. Is there anyone who irritates you, or anyone who just seems to eat up time you can't spare? How can you demonstrate gentleness and patience when you encounter that person?

18

GRACE FOR EACH OTHER

COLOSSIANS 3:13–14

There was a little girl who was invited to a slumber party. One of the other guests at the party began to make fun of her appearance. The young hostess found it easier to join in the teasing than to defend the girl being teased. The child had a terrible time and had to endure an entire night with girls who made her feel badly about herself. A few weeks later, the hostess invited the little girl for a play date. Another child was there, and again the little girl was mistreated and not defended by her hostess. But when she was invited over a third time, she still gladly accepted. Each time she was invited, the little girl chose to believe that her friend would treat her well, despite her track record. This little girl knew how to bear her friend's shortcomings and forgive her.

BEARING AND FORGIVING (COL. 3:13)

John Wesley once pointed out that to bear with each other is to withstand a person's present shortcomings, whereas to forgive is to have mercy for something that has happened in the past.[1] Forgiving is for grievances—that is to say, offenses committed. But bearing with a person is just understanding and loving them for who they are and where they are in their journey as a Christian.

We must remember that those who have unusual personalities (in our opinion, perhaps) were created according to God's design. He likes them that way! The onus is upon us to embrace them for themselves, trying to view them through God's eyes. Of course, some people are not just quirky; they are difficult. Though God doesn't want anyone to act in a purposefully contrary way, He does expect us to tolerate such people and treat them with respect. The truth is that everyone wants to be accepted and loved, and some of the oddest behavior is really just an awkward attempt to win favor.

We also bear with other Christians by helping them in their spiritual progress. Our role may well be to assist and even admonish, but never to judge or belittle others for their sins or their immaturity. I have seen Christians look down their noses at a brother or sister for a certain sin, when they had only recently rid themselves of that sin.

(I might say they replaced it with arrogance!) While we most certainly want to help others move into holier living, we dare not sit in the judgement seat. As Jesus said, "Do not judge, or you too will be judged" (Matt. 7:1). We should also note that not everyone is in the right position to speak admonishment into another person's life. Jesus taught us not to address the speck in a brother's eye if we have a plank in our own (see Matt. 7:3–5).

We are not only told to forgive whatever it is another person has done to us, but we are also told, "Forgive *as the Lord forgave you*" (emphasis mine). How and why did Christ forgive you? He forgave you fully. He forgave you because He loved you and wanted a relationship with you. It is inconsistent with Scripture to say that we should forgive others *for our own sake*, because it is the only way that *we ourselves* heal. That does not resemble the forgiveness of Christ. The only self-interest Christ had in forgiving us was restoring us to relationship with Himself, because He loved and desired us.

Conventional wisdom says, "Sam will feel healed if Sam forgives Jane." Sometimes it even goes a step further: "Once Sam has healed himself by forgiving Jane, he can move on with his life, distancing himself permanently away from Jane." If that even qualifies as forgiveness, it is certainly incomplete. God's wisdom says, "Sam must forgive Jane so that Jane is released from guilt. The two must continue on in a harmonious relationship, which is a gain for both." This task is harder.

One caveat must be given. God does not expect any of His children to remain in an ongoing, harmful relationship. God loves us and expects us to respect ourselves rather than plant ourselves right in the middle of something dangerous or toxic. In such a case, grant a genuine, loving forgiveness. Don't just forgive so that you feel better; forgive that person so that he or she is free from past guilt. But don't give that person the opportunity for new guilt. In other words, if your husband beats you, forgive what he has done—even if he doesn't ask for it. Look at him through the eyes of Christ and find compassion, and honestly forgive the past. But if he is not going to stop beating you, get away. Don't stand in his path, giving him opportunity to do more damage to your body and his own soul.

THE BINDING AGENT (COL. 3:14)

We're told that the thing that binds all the characteristics of the new self together is love. In the words of '80s rock star Howard Jones, "What is love anyway? Does anybody love anybody anyway?" It's not surprising he should ask such a question. The world doesn't really give us an accurate or even satisfying picture of what love is. It isn't passion.

It isn't just having fun together. It isn't possessiveness; it is never characterized by jealousy. What really is love?

First John 4:9 says: "This is how God showed his love among us: He sent his one and only Son into the world that we might live through him." Genuine love addresses the loved one's need over your comfort. Christ modeled that love in the very act of becoming human and of course in the way He lived and died. The nuts and bolts of Christlike love are listed in another of Paul's letters, 1 Corinthians. Chapter 13 of that book describes love as patient and kind, not envious, boastful or proud, not dishonoring, selfish or angry. On top of that, it doesn't keep track of offenses. Does this sound familiar? Does it sound like Colossians 3:12–13?

Imagine a patchwork garment. Each patch is specific, but together they form one garment. If we are to put on love, like a garment, then it is surely made of such a diverse yet unified cloth, with patches of the separate characteristics of kindness, humility, compassion, and so on. If one person forgives another but doesn't do it with kindness, what has really been achieved? Or, imagine a person who does something compassionate, but secretly regards herself as better than the person she is helping. Is compassion without humility really love?

Additionally, we must note that Colossians 3 tells Christians how to treat *other Christians*. Certainly we are to treat everyone with genuine love, but these verses have added significance because it matters even more how we treat those who are in fellowship with us. We are one body, together, united in Christ.

But why is it that we so often extend grace to people outside the body of Christ more readily than to our brothers and sisters? Why do we feel we have a right to sit in the seat of judgment against our own, and be so stingy with our forgiveness? How is it that we consider ourselves a higher court than the Holy One, who grants full forgiveness in measureless love? Scripture compels us to give thought to the way in which we treat one another.

A dear friend of mine fell into a particular sin that caused a fair amount of grief to the people in her life. Eventually she came to her senses and sought the Lord's forgiveness and the forgiveness of everyone she had hurt. She was humble and contrite, as was appropriate. Another friend in her life—a fellow Christian—had been particularly judgmental during the whole scenario. The sin had not been committed against him and didn't really touch his life in any way, but my friend extended an apology to him because he was quite disturbed by all that had happened. Verbally, he forgave her. But he never treated her the same again. In fact, he ostracized her. When they were both invited to the same party or wedding, she could not be at ease because of his snubs. She lost his friendship and the fellowship of his wife and children.

At worst, that's not forgiveness at all. At best, it's loveless forgiveness. It certainly isn't Christlike forgiveness, because Christ forgave so that guilt might be erased and so that He might enjoy relationship with us. Let us remember that we ourselves have been in dire need of forgiveness at times in our lives. And like Christ, may we forgive our brothers and sisters to the fullest extent.

REFLECTION QUESTIONS

1. What is the difference between bearing with someone and forgiving someone, according to this study?

2. Think of those people you've had to forgive in your life. Do you think your forgiveness has been complete?

3. What is the difference between guiding or admonishing someone and judging them? Are you in a position to admonish at this point in your spiritual walk?

4. Do you sit in judgment over anyone right now? If so, how can you take a step toward forgiveness?

5. Have you ever felt that a fellow Christian withheld their approval from you? What was that like, and what does it teach you about how to treat others?

19

WHO WE ARE TOGETHER

COLOSSIANS 3:15–16

The Salvation Army summer camps are staffed mostly by teenagers and young adults who are members of nearby Salvation Army congregations. When I was a teenager, I didn't work at summer camp like most of my church friends did because I had other commitments. I had multiple occasions to visit our camp during the summers, though. It was easy to see how much the staff members enjoyed each other. Throughout the rest of the year there would be lots of area-wide events for the Army, and I'd see staff members meet up and reconnect. I was an outsider to the important camp culture, and I longed to be part of it. They made so many memories together and seemed to build such a bond.

Every people group has its unique culture. I could look at the camp staff and characterize their relationships as fun-loving, caring, and deep. It looked meaningful; it looked like something worth belonging to.

The previous verses in Colossians 3 discussed how each of us should conduct ourselves in relationship to the group. They help us discover the identity of our new selves when we belong to Christ. However, here in verses 15 and 16 we begin to explore the identity of the group, rather than the individual. What should a worshiping body look like? If outsiders were to characterize us, what would we hope they would see? In this study, we'll explore how Paul described the identity of the church then—and what it means for us today.

AT PEACE WITH EACH OTHER (COL. 3:15)

My five children came in clumps. The first one was an only child until he was eight. Numbers two and three came in quick succession, just twenty months apart. When they were teenagers, we adopted our youngest—two biological half siblings who are one week shy of being exactly two years apart. Anyone who has raised children who are close in age knows what it is like to long for peace in the household. With our second and third, and now with our fourth and fifth, sometimes arguments seem to cause the whole house to vibrate. My husband and I cry out for peace! Peace between the siblings allows peace for the whole family.

One of life's great joys is a family at peace with each other. When the occasional arguments slack off, laughter and encouragement surface. Memories are made. My youngest asked me what my brother and sister and I fought about as children, and though I could remember that we had tiffs, I couldn't remember what they were about. My lasting memories are of the fun we had.

God longs to see His children living in harmony, enjoying and helping and building one another up. When misunderstandings happen, they should be dealt with and not result in permanent rifts between people. Don't we also hope for these things from our church bodies? Frankly, these are the things we should reasonably expect.

FILLED WITH GRATITUDE (COL. 3:15)

Paul told the Colossians as a group that they should be thankful. Remember that Christians are a group, the chosen ones,[1] who have received God's grace. No collective of people has more reason to celebrate, more reason to give thanks, than those who have received the grace provided by Christ's sacrifice and stand washed clean before their Father.

It's easy to forget to be grateful for what has been long enjoyed. To my horror, I once heard one of my children complaining that we had only brought two forms of electronic

177

entertainment for a three-hour road trip; the third device had been forgotten at home! I responded rather impatiently: "When I was a kid, we had books, and we looked out the window. And that was it!" I keep expecting today's kids to effuse gratitude for what they have. To me, things like smartphones and tablets are ever astonishing because we didn't have them when I was growing up. But for many kids this life is the only one they've known.

Like those of us who lived before cell phones and iPads and continue to marvel at them, those who met or re-found Christ after years of life without Him may find it easier to be grateful for the grace they've received. One of my sons was dramatically returned to faith as a young adult after wandering away from Christ for years. He is the most joyful, thankful person I've ever known. He is constantly telling everyone how good God is to him. Individuals who were saved as very young children and have been consistent in their Christian walk may not be as awestruck by the blessings of God. They can be taken for granted because they have been present in their lives for as long as they can remember.

Even so, anyone—the newly saved or the long-saved—may find their gratitude growing dim at times. We can't fault people for not counting their blessings when a loved one dies or their house gets robbed. We must give room for normal human emotion. But our churches should be places where a spirit of thankfulness causes a sense of deep joy—a joy that dwells deeper in our hearts than the pain life's circumstances can bring. Our church family should soothe temporary grief while reminding each other of what God has done for us.

CONSUMED WITH THE MESSAGE OF CHRIST (COL. 3:16)

When Paul told the Colossians to let the "message of Christ dwell among you richly," it is unclear whether he meant the gospel Christ Himself had taught, or the things Paul had been writing to the Colossians about Christ in this letter. But it really doesn't matter. The important thing is that the church is full of the truth about Christ and His grace. N. T. Wright says, "The church is to be stocked with good teaching as a palace is filled with treasures."[2] As Christ followers, we must soak in Christ's message while at the same time letting it flow from us freely.

When the the body of Christ lets the word of Christ dwell in them, they are prepared to involve themselves in each other's lives as teachers and admonishers. To *admonish* someone could be to reprimand or warn him or her. Faithful Christian leaders and friends do not stay silent when someone is entrapped in sin. At times in our church

179

life, someone may need to be taken to task—"called out," as some would say. But admonishing can also mean to warn someone about something potentially dangerous. This act of discipleship is one of the benefits of generational diversity in a worshiping body. Often the older are able to warn the younger based on life experience, though age is not always a factor.

In this passage, the admonishing and teaching are done in three distinct musical ways: psalms, hymns, and songs from the Spirit. Most likely, "psalms" refers to songs based on the Old Testament. "Hymns" would have been the new music sung by Christians that was used both to praise and also to teach Christian doctrine. "Songs from the Spirit" are believed to be spontaneous outpourings of musical praise, as led by the Spirit.

Today we have many types of Christian music. Some teach sound doctrine, like the hymns of Luther or Wesley. Others are an expression of praise and wonder with a posture of worship, like many of the songs of Matt Redman or Chris Tomlin. Perhaps many of us felt admonished by Redman's words: "I'm coming back to the heart of worship, and it's all about you, it's all about you Jesus."

Music is powerful. Years ago, when CDs were still the most popular way of consuming music, I put together a CD of a number of songs about the nearness of God when we hurt. I sent the CD to a friend when her husband died and to another when she suffered a different kind of personal pain. I knew that the words of the songs would penetrate their hearts, because great music can pave the way for a message to get through.

In verse 16, *The Voice* reads, "Keep on singing—*sing to God* from hearts *full and spilling over* with thankfulness." If the people of a church are full of gratitude and love each other, doesn't it make sense that they would sing together? Singing together is a tremendously unifying, beautifully human thing. Even the birds, with all their lovely music, are unable to assemble and sing the same song. We have been given a gift: to express our collective joy, our collective praise, our hope, our faith, etc.

Go to a baseball game, and you'll see people singing together. Go to a high school event; they have a school song. Go to a social justice rally and see how long it takes before someone breaks into either an old spiritual from the days of slavery or a John Lennon song. When people join together in favor of a team or school or a cause—anything that binds them together—they sing.

We can find no worthier cause nor more unifying force than the grace and love of God. And so, we sing!

REFLECTION QUESTIONS

1. Do you have peace in your church? If not, how do you think it should be handled?

2. Why is gratitude important?

3. The next time you sit down to a meal with a fellow Christian, take turns listing off three things for which you are grateful.

4. In what ways does your church dispense solid biblical teaching?

5. How can we use music to teach or admonish each other? Has it ever been used in that way in your life?

6. Can you remember a time when you were singing in church and you felt especially moved?

20

ALL IN THE NAME OF THE LORD JESUS

COLOSSIANS 3:17

Imagine what it must have been like to be a Colossian Christian. Imagine you were known in your community as someone who started following a new religion from a foreign land. You betrayed the gods of your people, and you hooked yourself up to something that didn't seem to have taken full shape yet. But the scales had dropped from your eyes! You knew that the gospel was true, and you wanted others to be led out of the futility of worshiping false gods and into the joy of knowing the one true God.

If this were your reality, you would find it very important to represent the Lord Jesus well. You would need to live out your new identity in Christ in a bold, noticeable way. You would have to remember at all times that you were the messenger of something new and beautiful, not only as you shared your faith, but also by the very way you lived.

REPRESENTING CHRIST

But isn't it the same now, for us? Even in the United States, which is considered by many other Western countries to be very religious, secularism has surpassed living a life based on an established faith system as the norm. A few decades ago most people had a basic understanding of what Christianity was about. But if you watch or read news today, you'll find Christians characterized in a way that feels rather foreign.

First, when news reporters talk about Christians, they talk about us as if we are a separate body to the side of regular life. Yes, we are a separate, holy chosen people. But in the past Christianity wasn't treated by others as something foreign to mainstream society. Second, the description of who we are, our character and our objectives, is quite disturbing. When secular outlets describe our faith, they often don't describe it as a religion of love or freedom. They portray Christianity as a system of harsh rules and particular biases.

Like the Colossians, we find ourselves in a society that doesn't understand us or our God. If the world is to increase its understanding of God, our responsibility is to make it happen. Paul instructs us to do everything "in the name of the Lord Jesus." To do something in someone's name means that you are his representative. In fact, we actually *bear* His name. We are "Christians"—"little Christs." This moniker, once given to Jesus' followers in order to tease and mock them, should be our constant reminder that the world is looking to us to see what Jesus is like. Acts 17:28 says that "in him we live and move and have our being." He is the source from which our lives spring, and we must faithfully portray His image in all we do.

When I was in college, an unsaved friend asked me about the behavior of one of his fraternity brothers. He was genuinely confused as to how this fellow student could behave wildly but still call himself a Christian. I can hardly blame him for his confusion! What a travesty it is for people to bear the name of Christ but live in a manner that does not represent Christ's values.

When I check the news, I hear reports of Christians aggressively pushing their views while treating those who disagree with their agenda in shockingly unloving ways. What a travesty it is for people to bear the name of Christ but live in a manner that does not represent Christ's love and mercy.

When I look at some of my friends and even myself, I see a hesitancy to share the gospel of freedom found in Christ with friends who do not know Him. Moments occur when our unsaved friends are open and searching, but we let the moments pass. What a travesty it is for people to bear the name of Christ but not represent who He is and what He has done for us.

IMITATING HIS CHARACTER

If whatever we do or say is to be done in Jesus' name, we must act and speak in ways that are congruous with His nature. And no one can imitate a character that they haven't studied. We can study the character of Christ through the written Word. We can also study His character when we are in prayer and His nature is revealed to us. The Lord is not hidden from us. If we are to be His true and faithful representatives in this world, we should really know His character and faithfully display it through our lives.

As a writer, I sometimes meet strangers who have read something that I've written, which is always a great delight for me. But my friends also read my work, and they often say, "Oh man, I could hear your voice when I read that." They know my personal inflections and tones and passions. My written work sounds like the person they know because we are in a relationship together. It is much the same with the Lord. The more time we spend knowing Him, the more we hear and recognize His voice. We recognize it in Scripture; we recognize it in prayer. We may even recognize it in nature and in music. The more we know Him, the more we hear Him. And the more we hear Him, the more we can imitate Him.

LIVING IN HIS PRINCIPLES

After teaching the Colossians that the old rituals and practices had been replaced by grace and freedom, Paul said *whatever you do* should be done in Christ's name. The New Testament is not full of lists of dos and don'ts. Because the grace of Jesus Christ allows us to be in intimate connection with God, we can know how to live in a way that pleases Him. We can decipher what is right, what is wrong, what is loving, what is good. We know these things because the books of the gospel and the rest of the New Testament teach the principles of our faith.

In the days of the Old Testament, many attempted to devise rules to cover every inevitability. But since Christ, the *principles* of love and grace and holiness are taught and parsed out for us, and we are to apply them to the situations we encounter. We are not left alone, however, to figure this out. We are guided by the Holy Spirit, and we have brothers and sisters to teach and admonish us.

One thing about living by principle instead of rule is that we have no loopholes. You can always find a loophole in a rule. But God calls us to live by the spirit of the law, not the letter of it. This method is freer, but sometimes it is harder. For example, a Christian must always be loving in her actions, because loving others is the principle Christ taught us. A Christian must also always watch his tongue, because verses such as Colossians 3:8 address the principle of loving speech. There are no exceptions. A principle is like a blanket. Everyone is covered by it.

GIVING THANKS

Paul ended this verse by telling the people to be thankful—again! Paul really drove this point home. But let's consider this instruction in the specific context of this verse. What is it that we have to be thankful for in relation to living principled lives in the name of Jesus Christ?

We can be thankful that we are under the grace of Jesus Christ, which has freed us from regulatory living and given us the opportunity to shine for Him because we bear His likeness. We can be thankful that through the Holy Spirit, and with each other's help, we are equipped to imitate the perfect Model that has been provided for us. It is an honor to be Christ's representative in this world, and we should be grateful for such an immense privilege.

REFLECTION QUESTIONS

1. How does society characterize Christians?

2. How do your unsaved friends characterize Christians?

3. In what ways are you a good representative of Christ? In what ways are you failing?

4. How do you spend time learning the character of Christ?

5. What change would you like to make in your life so that you are better at doing all things in the name of Jesus Christ?

21

THE HOUSEHOLD TABLES
PART 1

COLOSSIANS 3:18–21

In the early days of the church, the new Christians expected Jesus to return any day. As such, churches tended to be unstructured and undisciplined (which is why we see much structural and corrective information given in Paul's letters). Verses 18–24 of Colossians 3 form what Martin Luther called the "Haustafeln," or "household tables."[1] In these verses, Paul specified the roles and attitudes of members of a household. He was instructing the people of his day to live according to the structure of their society, but to do so in a way that would honor the Lord. Their mind-set toward members of the household had to be shifted.

The household tables (also known as "household codes") are all meant to show relationships that are reciprocal. Love is to permeate every Christian home. We have studied what love looks like, and it is far from domineering or pushy or insulting. In real love relationships, each person wants the other to flourish.

Before we dive into the household tables, let me point out one thing: Though slaves may have been common members of the Colossian Christian's household, they are not part of ours, so for our purposes we will consider verses 22–24 separately, in the next study.

HUSBANDS AND WIVES (COL. 3:18–19)

In the ancient Greek and Jewish societies, women were considered beneath men (though their status was a bit better among Greeks than Jews). In their prayers, Jewish men regularly thanked God that they had not been born as a woman. After Paul taught that there is neither Jew nor Greek, slave nor free, one might wonder why he used language that seemed to put the woman in her (downtrodden) place. Especially if you have read Galatians, where he wrote that there is neither "male nor female" in the body of Christ (see Gal. 3:28), you might find yourself wondering: Why would he now insist that women submit to their husbands?

Paul's writing certainly insisted on a change in the way Christians viewed and treated other people. As we have seen, all humanity enjoys equal status in Christ. While Paul pushed for change in perception and behavior, he did not advocate for Christians to overthrow the entire societal system. Certain structures were in place and accepted by the world. Christianity would not be well received if it were an upheaval of all that was known—including the marital relationship.

Think about how Jesus Himself related to women. His willingness to talk to and interact with women was unheard of. He liberated and dignified women in a way that no one had seen before. Yet, He did not insist on the obliteration of all societal norms. His life-changing conversation with the Samaritan woman at the well occurred in private. Because of their encounter, she was empowered; she was the first evangelist in the New Testament. Subtly, Jesus brought dignity to women. He did not sit on the mount and preach the overthrow of the male-dominated system of the day. And yet, He began to change that system by granting women a dignity they'd never known—one at a time.

Philosophers such as the Stoics and other groups, including the religious Jews, also had household tables. Paul was getting his readers back in line with accepted tables but was making important tweaks. Stoics based their codes on what they considered to be the law of nature. "As is fitting" was a phrase they commonly used. But observe Paul's nuance: wives were to submit to their husbands "as is fitting *in the Lord*." They were to do things *the Lord's way*.

The Lord requires all His believers to be humble, but not humiliated. He asks us to serve one another, but not set ourselves up for mistreatment. Thanks to Christianity, women were elevated in a new way. But Paul didn't stop there. In those days, marriages were generally made for reasons other than love. A marriage might provide economic gain. Or a man might simply require a woman so that he could have someone manage his home and give him children. No doubt many husbands and wives did grow to love each other, but what a wonderful thing it is that Scripture insists that love be the norm among Christian spouses.

Having just been taught what it was to be part of the new humanity as citizens of the kingdom of God, the husbands should have understood that their wives were as fully human as they were. All the teaching beforehand wasn't only for male-to-male relationships! Verses 5–14 should have made that perfectly clear! These parameters were in place not only when a woman "submitted" to her husband, but also when husbands in turn loved—not merely sexually, but in a godly way—their wives. Husbands were to treat their wives with respect.

In marital relationships today (as then), mutual respect is key. One person does not dominate the other. Kristina LaCelle-Peterson has an eye toward husband-wife relationships when she comments on 1 John 3: "You can't convincingly say, 'We are going to do things my way because I am the head of this house,' and in the next breath say, 'but I am ready to lay my life down for you.'"[2] One is selfish, one is selfless.

CHILDREN AND PARENTS (3:20–21)

In ancient Greek homes, the children were barely a step above servants. They were expected to be at the ready to accommodate the wishes of their fathers. They did not have a voice and obedience was expected. Paul's household codes provide a new perspective. Children were somewhat empowered by this code for the new humanity. They possessed the ability to please the Lord. This fact in itself—the fact that the Lord would enjoy them, make note of their conduct, and even approve of it—lifted the status of a child. On top of that, Paul made it clear that a father should not frustrate his child so that the child wouldn't lose heart. The development and feelings of a child mattered.

Today, children are often placed on pedestals. Families structure their lives around the child's schedule. Some parents are just as likely to ask their child's permission as they are to give instruction.

By putting directions for the conduct of both parents and children together in this passage, Paul shows us what an appropriate, balanced relationship looks like, where everyone is respected. Children are to be obedient; the adult is in charge. In this relationship, a child learns to live under authority—ultimately, God's authority.[3] And here, a child deserves to feel safe. He needs to be able to trust the person he must obey.

As a result, a parent should never physically harm his child. But Paul made it clear that a parent must be just as cautious with a child's psyche. A child is pretty powerless when treated unfairly. Although he may protest, at the end of the day the parents call all the shots. And if the parents are unfair or cruel, what recourse does a child have but to grow bitter? O'Brien translates the word as "provoke" rather than "embitter." What can a provoked child do? He does not have the power of an adult and must buckle under his parents' injustice. No wonder he would become "discouraged"!

So whether you have to reestablish authority in the life of your child or soften your approach toward your children, let it come from a place of love—first for God and then for your child.

The salient point in these household tables is that every person in the household should show respect and receive respect. We are talking about God's new order, where *every* person is to be regarded as an equal child of God.

REFLECTION QUESTIONS

1. Describe the household roles in your family of origin. How well do you think they lined up with God's desire for equality and mutual respect?

2. Not everyone will agree on the roles of husband and wife. What is your understanding, and how do you think Scripture supports it? Are you able to see how a person might read Scripture and come up with a different view?

3. If you are a parent of children in the home, how do you feel you treat them? Are your children being taught to obey, and are you refraining from provoking them?

22

THE HOUSEHOLD TABLES
PART 2

COLOSSIANS 3:22—4:1

Let's be honest. We twenty-first-century Christians would be a lot more comfortable if the Bible came right out and condemned slavery. But it doesn't do that. In fact, not only does it tell slaves how to conduct themselves, but it also addresses *masters*. The implication here is that some Christians were slave owners, and Paul did nothing to stop it.

By all accounts, slavery in the first century was a much larger societal structure than it was even in American history. The whole economy and the management of a vast population depended upon it. To us, anywhere slavery is to be found, the only appropriate response is to demand its full and immediate dismantling. Though it is strange to say it, the first-century Christians might not have agreed. We won't pretend that slavery was pleasant in those days. While some slaves were given authority, even running businesses for their masters, others were treated abysmally. All slaves were property and did not have any rights over their own lives, nor any other rights that a citizen would have had. So why not call for abolition? Two scholars give us a glimpse into first-century realities:

[W]e should respect the limitations of what could be said in urging both slaves and owners to maintain the social order. The incitement to revolt would have been suicidal, as the earlier slave uprisings, led by Spartacus in 73–71 B.C.E., had shown.[1]

Think of the social chaos that would have resulted from setting free millions of slaves. What would these people do, and how would they be fed? Slavery was a means of maintaining peace and order in the empire; the abolition of this institution would have led to political and economic chaos.[2]

Arthur Patzia also reminds us that Christians believed Christ would return at any point, and in Him everyone was/would be free, and so "since they had no mandate from God to overthrow the world, they lived peaceably in the assurance that the last days were near."[3] (Living peaceably *was* a mandate in the New Testament letters; see Rom. 12:18.) Because Christ did not appear quickly, Paul realized he needed to give rules for household behavior, and as has been said before, Paul knew that God wanted His people to function within society, not turn society on its ear.

These points may seem more like excuses than valid reasons; they may not be much of a comfort to us. Perhaps we like it better when Jesus overturned the merchant tables in the temple as a reaction to their unjust extortion of the poor than when He met privately with the woman at the well, delivering her from oppression and empowering her in unprecedented ways. We want action. We want justice. We want a revolution. But sometimes the plan of the Lord is slow and steady.

A MATTER OF THE HEART (COL. 3:22)

One of the things we've seen in Colossians is that God is more concerned about what stems from the heart than He is about us constructing and following rules. He requires the slave to have the *heart* of a servant and the master to have a *heart* of equality, not superiority.

This ideology is a revolution of a whole different kind. Civilizations set rules that force people to treat each other fairly—and that is good. But here we must allow for the fact that Paul was neither advising how to set up an earthly, human civilization nor how to overthrow one. Rather, he

201

was giving instruction on how to have the heart of a citizen of the coming kingdom while living in this present world.[4]

THE ROLE OF SLAVES AND MASTERS
(COL. 3:23; 4:1)

The fact that Paul addressed slaves in his letter was no small thing. They were given instruction just like fathers and masters, because they were equal in the sight of God. They were part of the body of worshipers who received the letter, and they were fully acknowledged by Paul as part of the church family.

So what instruction did Paul give?

Slaves were to obey at all times, not only when they were being watched. Diligent work was to be done with a sincere heart, in a manner that honored the Lord. There is an old story about a young household servant in the late nineteenth century who was saved under the ministry of The Salvation Army. Her explanation about the change in her life went something like this: "Before I got saved, I used to sweep the dirt under the carpet. Now I'm saved, I clean it all the way up." What a simple, lovely testimony of the difference that Christ makes in our attitudes.

Just about every human in the world falls under someone else's authority at some level. Most of us have tasks to complete, whether filing taxes under authority of the government or cleaning the grill when employed at a fast food place. The true test of our character comes with how we conduct ourselves when no one would be the wiser if we cheated or were careless.

The motive behind such assiduous work is that it is not done for the sake of the master, but for the sake of the Master! It is very freeing to understand that all that we do, we do to please God. When human bosses or governors or principals are less than fair or kind, we can easily be discouraged. But in these moments, we can remember that every effort we make is to the Lord, for the Lord. Let us take heart and let us labor faithfully, for the Lord is glorified and pleased when we do.

The command wasn't really any different for masters (4:1). They too were to work to please the true Master, and He—maker and lover of *all* humankind—would not take kindly to seeing any part of humanity treated unjustly. Colossians 3 has taught us to love our Christian brothers and sisters and understand them as our equals in the sight of God. It is safe to assume that no one reading this book has any slaves. But we may have people under our authority. Remember that the Master attends to how every person is treated, even those who rank lowest in our society.

THE INHERITANCE (COL. 3:24–25)

The slaves were reminded that because they were children of the Lord, they would receive an inheritance from Him. A slave could not inherit anything from his master. This promise of an inheritance meant that the slave was embraced as a full son or daughter of God. The inheritance would come after death and would be eternal. Such a promise would certainly buoy the hopes of those who had no possibility of any gain or advancement on earth, and whom society considered outsiders of the household.

Though the promise of inheritance is for the eternal future, we may assume that the warning that those who don't behave rightly will be repaid for it is applicable to this life. Paul said in other epistles that even believers will stand before the Lord on the day of judgment (see Rom. 14:10; 1 Cor. 4:5), but if people who belong to Christ (to whom this letter is addressed) are going to be "repaid for their wrongs," it will not be in the form of some punishment in the next life. Grace is poured over those who are saved; they will not pay an eternal penalty for individual sins. Rather, this verse seems to indicate that if a slave doesn't serve his master well, he can expect some sort of repercussion in this life, and that is as the Lord would have it.[5] Christian slaves were not to decide that because—they and their masters were brothers in the Lord—and they could slack off on their work.

We too may be assured that we will receive an inheritance from the Lord, because we are His children. Like our ancient brothers and sisters, any poor behavior on our part will have repercussions, often in the form of broken relationships. Let us live as equals in Christ, knowing no favoritism, and honoring Him in all we do, whether as slave or master.

REFLECTION QUESTIONS

1. How did Christianity bring a new sense of dignity to slaves?

2. Imagine how the dynamics in an ancient household would change if master and slave both became Christians. How did your relationships change when you were saved (if you weren't a young child)?

3. Have you ever been or are you now in a difficult situation with someone in authority? If you remember to do your work for Christ, how might that change your approach?

4. What eternal promise is found in this Scripture, and what do you think it means for you?

23

PRAYER

COLOSSIANS 4:2

My friend Erica shared a story about the prayer life of her mother, Joanne. When Joanne was a young wife and mother the family lived in North Pole, Alaska, about twenty miles outside of Fairbanks. She was alone in an isolated three-story log cabin in the woods every day with no phone. She decided to teach herself to sew. She started making flannel shirts for her husband, but struggled to get the sleeves right. She spent hours in her little sewing nook trying to master them. One day she finally achieved her goal. As Erica put it, "She held up the sleeve and turned to her left and exclaimed proudly and out loud to Jesus, "Look! I did it!" Erica went on to say, "That's how close they'd become during those trying and frustrating days at home. He'd been there all along."

Prayer is a door swung wide open to allow us relationship with God. Our prayer life should be like Joanne's—

consistent and intimate. And it should be chock-full of gratitude.

DEVOTED

Many Christians are blessed enough to receive salvation in the early years of life. Churches are peppered with saints who may have slipped a little now and again but have been mostly faithful their whole lives. That is truly something to celebrate!

But I can't help but offer a word of caution: Gratitude can easily get lost, especially with those who have been disciples of Christ for a very long time. We may forget what an incomprehensible marvel it is that we have the ability to talk to Almighty God, maker of all that was and is and ever will be, ruler over every universe that may be out there, the only true God, in whom all life has its origin. *We can talk to Him.* He hears me when I address Him from my family room couch each morning and from my bed each night, and every place in between. He hears you when you are praying in your car or at your desk or on your knees at the altar. We should never get over how incredible this unwarranted privilege is.

Even more, we don't have to force God to listen to us. I confess that as a mother I am not always completely attentive to my children. When I'm busy or in deep thought, I may or may not fully hear what my kids are telling me. And sometimes, honestly, I don't even want them to talk to me. I may want a little space. I may want a little peace and quiet. But God never tires of hearing us speaking to Him.

Verse 2 tells us to "devote" ourselves to prayer. Some translators use the word *persevere* instead of *devote*, which is a little bit closer to the Greek word in the original text. It means to persist in something, to be absorbed by it. So not only does God want to hear from us, but He also wants to hear from us *a lot*. If I were to make my own paraphrase, I would say, "Be obsessed with praying." God desires it.

Everyone knows what it is like to speak to someone who is not paying full attention. Even when on the phone with a friend, you can easily tell whether they are multitasking by their tone or the delay of their responses. It hurts to know that the person to whom you're speaking isn't fully engaged. But what a gift it is when someone is completely dialed in to you, eager to hear all that you say! I remember the way my father used to listen to the stories of my day and roll his eyes and laugh. I remember how he took delight in me.

Even more so, God delights in each of us. Despite the fact that God knows what we're thinking at all times, we are commanded to pray. It doesn't matter whether we speak out loud or direct our thoughts to Him, it just matters that we address Him. That we purposefully share our hurts, concerns, joys, and requests. That we turn to Him and ask for strength. That we let Him know we await His direction for our lives.

WATCHFUL

Paul gave instructions for prayer. The first is that the person praying should be "watchful" in prayer. There are two possible meanings here:

1. The Colossians were to watch for the return of the Lord, because it was imminent. Their prayers should be mindful of His return.
2. In the garden of Gethsemane, Jesus commanded Peter, James, and John to "watch and pray" so that they wouldn't fall into temptation. Jesus was warning them of the temptation at hand—to betray Him, which Peter did—and directing them to fight off temptation through prayer. The meaning in Colossians, then, would be to stay on the alert and to pray against the temptation that may come.

The first of these two seems unlikely. We have seen in chapter 3 that Paul gave instructions for households because it was becoming clear that Christ might not return as quickly as they had expected. Still, it is always appropriate to live as though today might be the day of His coming.

The second option is simple to apply to ourselves. Temptation is a regular part of the Christian's life. Even Jesus Himself faced it. We must be constantly on vigil, aware of the next one we may encounter. In our prayer life, we are to suit ourselves up in the necessary armor to combat temptation. Our prayers should not be just a list of requests. They should even include more than thanksgiving and praise. In our persistent, "obsessive" prayer we should be muscling up, making game plans against sin, and allowing ourselves to be chastised and reformed.

THANKFUL

The second instruction given is to be thankful. This is the sixth time in the small book of Colossians that Paul gave this directive. It was always frankly put, requiring no qualification. In this case, Paul doesn't even provide much context to attach it to. Just, when you pray, be thankful.

As this command to be thankful is the final of six and is found at the tail end of the book, let's consider it as instruction to look back through the letter of Colossians and review all that we have to be thankful for. Colossians begins with teaching the identity of Christ and proceeds to explain our new identity in Him. As all of that unfolds, there is much for which we can give thanks. Here are a few things:

- We have a hope stored up in heaven.
- We are part of the inheritance of His holy people.
- We have been rescued from darkness and brought into the kingdom.
- The Son is the image of the invisible God; the fullness of God dwells within Christ Jesus.
- Christ is the head of the church.
- Once enemies of God, we are now reconciled.
- God has disclosed the great mystery; Christ resides in Gentiles as well as believing Jews.
- Our old self has been put away.
- Once dead, we are now alive in Christ and our debt has been paid.
- Christ triumphed over powers and authorities through the cross.
- We are not subject to strict rules of ritual observance.
- Our life is hidden with Christ in God.
- All God's people are equal; there are no divisions or hierarchies.
- We are God's chosen and He dearly loves us.
- We can live in loving harmony with each other.
- Everyone in a household matters and deserves respect.

All the things above are worth celebrating. And how much more has He done—for His people as a whole, and for His people individually? That list has no end.

Let us be thankful.

REFLECTION QUESTIONS

1. How often do you pray, and what kinds of things do you pray about?

2. What can being watchful in prayer mean in your life?

3. Above is a list of things in Colossians for which we should be thankful. Put the verse numbers next to the bulleted points. As you hunt through the book to find the verse numbers, you may find things you wish to add to the list.

24

PRAY FOR US

COLOSSIANS 4:3–4

Paul asked the Colossians to pray "for us." Because he mentioned the company of Timothy at the beginning of the book, the "us" probably includes him. Timothy was a beloved ministry partner to Paul and may have also been imprisoned at the time. Paul was probably also making reference to people he mentions in the later verses. Aristarchus was a prisoner along with him, but the others likely were not—they were his companions in ministry in the larger picture. Most likely he was in contact with them as they came to tend to his needs.

MISSION FIRST (COL. 4:3–4)

It is commendable and so typical of Paul that his request was that they would have opportunities to spread the gospel. I suspect most of us would list being released from prison as our number one prayer request. But Paul was a single-minded man. He didn't even ask to be released from his chains so he could spread the gospel far and wide. He wanted to tell the good news and it seems as though he was content to do that where he was; he only wanted opportunities.

In Philippians 4:12, Paul wrote: "I know what it is to be in need, and I know what it is to have plenty. I have learned the secret of being content in any and every situation, whether well fed or hungry, whether living in plenty or in want."

The same attitude was present in Colossians 4:3–4. He considered his situation and his comfort to be irrelevant. This man, who was full of thanksgiving, did not live for himself, but lived for his Lord. Surely one can find tremendous freedom in such a life—not to fuss over what one has or doesn't have. Paul's trust was in God; his eye was on the eternal inheritance.

Paul modeled the desire to preach the message anywhere, anyway. That message is the "mystery of Christ," which we discussed in studies 6 and 7: that Christ dwells in His believers, and both Jews and Gentiles are welcome into His kingdom. The message has never changed. Christ invites all people, with no distinction, into His kingdom.

When one of my children was young, he explained to me that he felt it would be rude to talk about his belief in Christ to his Muslim friend because his friend believed something different. Another one of my children told me that sharing with a friend about Jesus would be completely unacceptable because that friend never went to church. I was disheartened; I thought I had taught my children that it was important to share their faith. But they live in a society that teaches that if we believe in equality, and if we are sensitive to the rights of others, we won't "push" our beliefs on people. However, if we truly believe that Christ is the light of the world and that He is the sole mediator between God and man, how can we not share it? Mocking others for believing something different, coercing, or belittling have no place in properly sharing the gospel. But the gospel is to be shared.

I think most Christians, if asked, would say that they are deeply concerned that the gospel be delivered to all people. But do we faithfully do it? Why should we not be as committed as Paul? In the Western world very little is at stake for us if we share what we believe, and yet we sit idly by while people we call our friends live without the joy of knowing Christ and die in their sin. On the day of judgment, no one gets the opportunity to point to someone else and say, "It's his fault I didn't believe!"—and yet, we are commanded by Christ to preach the gospel (see Matt. 28:19–20). No believer in Christ can reasonably deny that it is her obligation (and privilege) to tell others about the one true Lord.

Paul prayed for an open door to share the message; our lives are full of open doors. Most of us have relationships in many aspects of our lives, but we neglect to see our friends and acquaintances as people who need Jesus. I have often been astonished to learn how eager some of my unsaved acquaintances are to talk about faith issues, and equally surprised to learn how little they know sometimes. If we are available for open discussion in which neither party is ashamed to admit when they don't know something, people can move closer to Christ. If we genuinely care about someone, or genuinely care about humanity at all, we will not be silent about the most important thing we could possibly share with them—the love and grace God offers to us all.

LOUD AND CLEAR (COL. 4:4)

Finally, just as Paul hoped that he proclaimed the message clearly, we should pray the same thing for ourselves. Few of us can answer every theological challenge that comes our way. But with the Holy Spirit moving through us we are equipped to do the job that needs to be done. The household servant mentioned in study 22 didn't need to wax eloquent to get the point of the gospel across. She simply needed to testify to the difference it made in who she was.

I have repeatedly experienced how the Holy Spirit interprets the words we say for the benefit of the listeners. People often approach me after a sermon to tell me what the main takeaway was for them. Three people (for example) may apply three completely separate points to their lives, and a fourth may quote back to me something I never even realized I said. The Holy Spirit takes our words, even when they are fumbling and inadequate, and refines them into what thirsty hearts need to hear.

One of the beloved quotes in Christianity is: "Preach the gospel at all times. If necessary, use words." No doubt that when this was first uttered the point was that the way we live should be consistent with the gospel we claim. But it has been twisted to mean that we rarely ever need to verbally share the gospel because our lives will demonstrate all that people need to know. Such a notion really doesn't square with Paul's commitment to *"proclaim* it clearly" (emphasis mine). I can live a kind, good, upstanding life—but my neighbor who doesn't know Christ lives the same way. How does my life teach the gospel any more than hers does? Our actions must support our message, but when the door is open, the message must be proclaimed.

REFLECTION QUESTIONS

1. Paul wouldn't let even imprisonment be an excuse for not proclaiming the gospel. Do you have any excuses you allow yourself for not sharing the gospel with people you know? What are they?

2. Is there anyone in your life who might be receptive to hearing the gospel from you, or at least having a talk about faith?

3. What are your thoughts on the quote: "Preach the gospel at all times. If necessary, use words"?

25

FINAL ADVICE

COLOSSIANS 4:5–6

The television show *The Office* had a character named Angela who was supposed to be a Christian. Angela was always sour faced. She was judgmental and unkind. She was obsessed with regulations and she never let her hair down. She displayed an insufferable air of superiority in her attempts to be right and virtuous. If Angela were a real person and she invited someone to church with her, I can't imagine that anything would tempt that person to say yes. No one would want to be around her, and no one would be willing to go to the place where such unappealing traits were nurtured.

Unfortunately, many people would argue that Angela is a realistic representation of a Christian. Believing that, they are turned off to Christ because of what they understand His followers to be. Paul advised us to present ourselves

in a way that would draw others in, not push them away—
something he demonstrated in the way he lived.

WISDOM AND OPPORTUNITY (COL. 4:5)

Colossians 3 had much to say about how Christians
should treat each other. It is no surprise that the Lord also
cares immensely about how we treat "outsiders." But what
is it to "be wise in the way you act"? Why is it important
to "make the most of every opportunity"?

We can find a wonderful example in Acts 17, beginning
with verse 16. Paul was in Athens, teaching in the synagogue
about Jesus. Some of the philosophers of the city were interested in what he had to say, so they brought him to the
Areopagus—a forum of philosophers—to engage him in discussion. Paul began by commending them for their religiosity.
He called attention to their altar "to an unknown god" and
proceeded to reveal the truth of the one real God. He did not
mock them for their ignorance, nor did he condemn them as
pagans. He realized that their altar was an attempt to find the
truth, and he fulfilled that pursuit for them.

In his discourse he quoted Athenian poets, respecting
their insight. He wisely showed respect for their scholars.
He was familiar with Athenian teaching and with their
manner of debate. He made the most of the opportunity by

playing by the established rules of the community, engaging with the Areopagus in the customary way.

Some laughed at Paul. Others said that they would like to hear more from him later. But some were won over by his sound argument and became believers. And that is why it is important to use every opportunity: some may be won to Christ. Lives may be changed forever.

Our efforts to proclaim the gospel will be met with mixed reactions, too. It is not a failure on our part if we present our faith to others and they wish to ruminate on it a while, or even if they flatly reject it. We are responsible for the presentation of the message. Conviction is the job of the Holy Spirit, and repentance is the job of the hearer.

From the scene in Acts 17 we can learn to speak respectfully about and to others, and to work within a manner that is acceptable to them. Most people come to faith because a friend shared with them at an opportune moment. That friend had emotional currency with the nonbeliever, making it socially acceptable to share what he believed. Few people come to faith because someone showed up at a football game with a sign that said "John 3:16." I'm not going to say it never happens. But it would be awfully rare. In my decades as a Christian, I have yet to hear that testimony.

Why doesn't the sign-at-a-sporting-event method lead to conversions? Because a relationship doesn't exist there, and to push your point outside the context of relationship is not generally considered acceptable. The person trying to share is often regarded as a fool because he works outside the parameters of normal interaction.

GRACE AND SALT (COL. 4:6)

A church near mine constantly posts angry, politically charged words from a liberal viewpoint on its reader board (church sign). They use Scripture to back up what they are saying, but it's like being bludgeoned with a Bible club. So what if they make a good point? The presentation is so self-righteous that it is never going to appeal to the outsider—especially one with a differing view. Nothing about this tactic is gracious, nor is it an appropriate way to answer the questions people may raise. The very fact that it is on a reader board means that the people who see it can't even engage in a conversation about the incendiary statements. Again, lack of relationship doesn't lead to anything fruitful. Why not use the reader board to say loving and kind things, which no one would object to reading on their way to work?

Graceful speech—kind, polite, thoughtful verbal interaction—is a gift to others. To do it well we must give others our full attention, undistracted by a smartphone or multitasking. By definition, it involves charm, tact, and compassion. Scripture instructs us to honor one another above ourselves (see Rom. 12:10), and graceful speech is one way in which that is done. It says, "I will speak to you in a respectful way, because you are worthy."

Our speech is gracious when it is "seasoned with salt." Salt's most important property, especially in the ancient world, was that it preserved food. Our speech should also be a preservative. It should preserve the dignity, the reputation, and the self-respect of others at all times. When a person walks away from a conversation with a Christian, she should walk away feeling good about herself because she has been uplifted by the respect she's received.

I remember when a young man who was living with us put his sneakers in our brand-new dryer. When I came home from work and found them tumbling around, I was livid. I hadn't even read the directions for the machine yet. I didn't know whether or not it could withstand such treatment. When he came in the front door I stomped angrily up to him and told him how very upset I was. I usually shy away from arguments, but I was mad. I was ready to go toe-to-toe.

Then he opened his mouth. I don't know if I've ever heard a person respond to anger with such gentleness. "I'm so very sorry," he said. "I had no right to do that. Please forgive me. Is there anything I should do now to fix things?"

His infraction wasn't horrible, and I was out of line. But his gracious answer to me was like nothing I expected. I was completely caught off guard. I have never forgotten that moment because I felt so heard, so understood, and so respected. I already had a high opinion of him, but his courteous response to me made me esteem him all the more.

That's the power of gracious speech. The recipient is open to hear what is being said because he doesn't feel threatened. He realizes that, in the other person's opinion, he has intrinsic value.

REFLECTION QUESTIONS

1. What kind of approach led you to Christ?

2. Do you feel you miss opportunities to share the gospel? Why?

3. Who is the most graceful speaker you know? Why do you view them that way?

4. How would you rate your own speech or approach when you discuss faith matters with others?

26

GODLY FRIENDSHIPS

COLOSSIANS 4:7–9

As a Salvation Army officer (pastor), I am blessed to have colleagues (including my husband) who understand what God has tasked me to do and are ever ready to lend emotional and prayer support. I have also turned to my colleagues for ministry advice and theological opinions. It's been tremendously helpful. But this is our profession, and we expect it from one another.

Every Christian, however, is (or should be) involved in mission. I wonder to what extent those who aren't in full-time ministry turn to each other for strength and support in their mission. I'm not referring to sharing personal problems and praying for each other, though that is important. I mean, do Christians depend on one another as they fulfill their ministry at work or school or in the neighborhood? What would such support look like?

It often seems to me that Christian friendship is an opportunity lost. Yes, we have friends who are fellow Christians. But do we work together as fellow servants of the Lord? More likely, we are as swimmers in a pool. We are in the same race, and we are side-by-side, but we stick to our own lanes. We may worship beside each other. We may pray for each other. But do we do ministry together, or find ways to inform and help each other in our respective missions? Maybe, when it comes to Christians living together on mission, we have something to learn from Paul and his support team.

TYCHICUS (COL. 4:7–8)

Tychicus, who hailed from the province of Asia (see Acts 20:4), was a devoted friend and colleague to Paul. He had accompanied Paul on journeys, Paul had commissioned him for at least one journey without him, and he had delivered letters for Paul. It is easy to detect Paul's fondness for him in the way he described him: dear brother (true believer), faithful minister (one whose life was dedicated to spreading the gospel), and fellow servant (who submitted his entire life to the Master, as Paul did).

Spreading the gospel in the first century was a gargantuan task. The world was a big place and modes of transportation were limited. Traveling had its perils, especially in Paul's case. Furthermore, the Christian faith was new; it had to be taught to people with no prior knowledge of its tenets (especially the Gentiles), and once converts were made, they had to be trained in the ways of Christian living.

In the middle of the twentieth century, Father Vincent Donovan moved to Tanzania, where he shared the message of Christianity with the Masai people. It was the first time they had heard anything about the gospel, anything about the true God. Early on, Donovan realized that his task as the first missionary to the Masai "was a role that would require every talent and insight and skill and gift and strength I had, to be spent without question, without stint"[1] because he did not know their culture, and they did not know his gospel.

It would have been the same for Paul. Certainly, companions in mission would have been highly valued. Sometimes the people of the first century who were tasked with establishing Christianity fell out with each other. But Tychicus was someone on whom Paul could rely.

ONESIMUS (COL. 4:9)

The Onesimus that is delivering this letter to the Colossians is the same Onesimus from the book of Philemon—the runaway slave who had been converted. Piecing all the bits together, scholars believe that Onesimus and Tychicus were carrying both the epistle to the Colossians and the letter to Philemon on the same trip. Philemon lived in the region of Colossae, if not in Colossae itself.

The letter Paul had written to Philemon explained that the slave had come under Paul's teaching and had become a believer, as was Philemon himself. In fact, Philemon hosted a home church. Paul told Philemon that the formerly useless slave had become useful to him and could be useful to Philemon once again, if only Philemon would receive him as a brother in Christ. (Paul engaged in a little wordplay on the name "Onesimus"—a common name for a slave, meaning "useful.") The people of Colossae would have been aware of Onesimus' crime, and it was helpful that Paul commended him to them as a "faithful and dear brother."

It is significant that a slave who had given his life to Christ was carrying a letter that emphatically taught that all people are equal in the kingdom of God. Anyone who may have looked down his nose at Onesimus when he arrived would have felt chastised upon reading the letter and would have had to make an attitude adjustment.

It is characteristic of the Lord that when He dismantles our old notions, He gives us the chance to put new lessons into practice. If you have someone you don't care to be around, don't be surprised if you are put on the same project together at work or in the same small group at church. The Lord may be orchestrating an opportunity for you to clothe yourself with love, having just studied Colossians 3!

THE JOB AT HAND (COL. 4:8–9)

Tychicus and Onesimus were to give a report about Paul (and Timothy) and to encourage the hearts of the Colossians. These verses read as though Paul thought the report of his condition would in itself encourage the Colossians. How could "Paul is still in prison" be encouraging news?

While I'm sure the Colossians would have loved to hear that God had delivered him from his chains, they could gather much strength in the report about Paul. Though in chains, he was full of thanksgiving and insisted that the Colossians also be thankful. He wrote words of deliverance and beauty about the Colossians' new identity and how they should now live. Despite his circumstance, he lauded the Lord Jesus and explained His deity and power to the recipients. Paul was more than okay; he was walking in holiness and radiating joy.

If Paul could do all that while languishing in prison, then surely the Colossians could use his epistle to sort out and move past the heresy that had been tripping them up. And certainly they, in their comfortable state compared to Paul's, could develop themselves as people of love, abandoning prior attitudes and ingrained prejudices.

Paul considered whatever happened to him to be for the greater good (see Rom. 8:28). He had "learned the secret of being content in any and every situation, whether well fed or hungry, whether living in plenty or in want" (Phil. 4:12), which was doing all things through the strength of Christ. Can we say the same?

REFLECTION QUESTIONS

1. What is your mission? Are other Christians a part of it? If not, should they be?

2. Have you ever had to receive and forgive someone who wronged you? How did the Lord help you through that experience?

3. Have you ever been angry with God over a situation in your life? What was Paul's attitude, and how could you apply the same attitude?

27

THE JEWISH COMPANIONS

COLOSSIANS 4:10–11

In verses 10–11 Paul passes on greetings from the three of his companions who are Jews: Aristarchus, Mark, and Jesus, also called Justus. This is the only mention of Jesus called Justus in Scripture, so we don't really know anything else about him. However, we can take a more in-depth look at Paul's other companions and discover what we can learn from their example.

ARISTARCHUS (COL. 4:10)

Aristarchus was seen at Paul's side a few times in the book of Acts. It has been suggested that he may have been a volunteer prisoner when Paul wrote Colossians. That is to say, he may have opted to become a prisoner with Paul, to serve and support him. It's a shocking level of devotion, but perhaps after three shipwrecks, a stoning, beatings, and many more life-threatening troubles that he had endured, Paul, in his early sixties, was not in great shape and really needed such a friend.

It is also suspected that Paul struggled with poor eyesight, his possible famous "thorn in the flesh." If that were the case, his eyesight would have been deteriorating even further with age. Therefore, a friend like Aristarchus may have been much needed, both in terms of friendship and in mission.

MARK (COL. 4:10)

Mark is the most interesting character in the list of companions. This man is John Mark, the same man who went on a mission with Paul and Barnabas and abandoned them, as told in Acts 15. Later, Paul and Barnabas discussed going on another trip, a tour to visit their converts in many cities. Barnabas was determined to take John Mark so that he might have the chance to prove his fidelity. But Paul disagreed so strongly that the two parted company and went on different mission trips, with Paul taking Silas this time. Acts does not mention that Barnabas and Mark were cousins, and this piece of information adds another layer of interest to the Acts story. This connection may also help explain why Barnabas was more eager to give Mark another try than Paul was.

However, time passed, and Paul was reunited with John Mark. The Colossians were aware of Mark's damaged reputation, and Paul insisted that if he came to visit them, they should welcome him. We do not have any record of whether or not such a visit ever took place. But again, as in the last study, we see that the Colossians would have been challenged to make good on their new faith according to the principles described to them in chapter 3, where Paul taught about forgiveness and peace between the people of God.

We can learn several lessons from the John Mark scenario. First, sin generally has a larger impact than we imagine it will. The city of Colossae was not even in the province of Pamphylia, where John Mark had deserted Paul and Barnabas. Yet Paul's special instruction regarding him seems to indicate that his reputation had spread all the way to Colossae.

Anyone who has tarnished her own reputation, or has had it unfairly tarnished, knows how quickly word spreads and how deep the damage can be. Really, sin of any type spreads its tentacles and causes harm beyond what we anticipate. We should not be surprised when it does.

The second lesson is that even our heroes can let us down. Paul, arguably the greatest hero of the Christian faith (besides Jesus), was not quick to forgive in Acts 15. One can imagine that as Paul sat in prison, being visited and tended to by Mark, he was keenly aware of his own past failing when it came to forgiveness. Any pastor's most effective sermons are the ones that touch upon something he himself needed to hear, or something she has struggled through in her own life. When Paul wrote to the Colossians about forgiving and bearing with each other, the words must have resonated in his own heart first. Like the rest of us, Paul made mistakes and continued to grow throughout his life. Even he was never a completed work.

The third lesson is that we must be able to look upon people as they are now, not as what they once were. My husband and I have a dear friend who is the resident manager of our transitional home for men who have finished The Salvation Army drug and alcohol rehabilitation program. When residents talk about their pasts in active addiction, our friend always says, "I don't know that man."

Recently, many of the men posted pictures on Facebook of what they looked like in active addiction and what they look like now. The difference was jaw-dropping. When a person is made new by Christ, whether it is for the first time or whether he or she is returning to Christ, we can't always physically see the difference. But let us put on our spiritual eyes and see that they are not who they were before, and it is senseless to regard them by their previous reputation.

The last lesson is that forgiveness is available for those who have gone astray. I don't know why John Mark left the mission in Pamphylia. Scripture does not tell us. But it doesn't matter. What matters is that whatever foolish move one makes, the Lord's arms are always open wide for the return of the prodigal. Fellow believers will forgive as well, if they are true to the Word. People who say, "I can't go back; not after what I've done" should be encouraged by the story of John Mark. There is always forgiveness. There is always a chance to start again.

It is a blessing that Mark is mentioned in this passage because it brings a beautiful end to a story that was left unfinished in Acts. Paul and Mark were reunited as brothers in Christ, and Mark was restored to the greater fold.

REFLECTION QUESTIONS

1. What's the greatest personal sacrifice you've ever made on behalf of a friend? Is there a brother or sister in Christ whose life would be made better *now* if you made some sort of sacrifice?

2. I've suggested four lessons that can be learned from the story of John Mark. Which of these lessons speaks most to your life, and why?

28

THE GENTILE COMPANIONS AND NYMPHA

COLOSSIANS 4:12–15

Epaphras evangelized, Luke wrote a gospel, Nympha opened her home for worship. It is exciting to think about how God used the personalities, skills, and possessions of the first Christians to start the Christian church. What thrilling days those must have been! Even now, the church moves forward and when we are actively spreading the gospel God uses us, too, in exciting ways. As you read about these ancient brothers and sisters, think about your own role in the church.

EPAPHRAS (COL. 4:12–13)

Epaphras doesn't get a lot of attention these days, but he was an important missionary. Once converted and theologically trained by Paul, he spread the gospel in his home city of Colossae and throughout the whole Lycus Valley. He was responsible for the founding of the churches in Colossae, Laodicea, and Hierapolis.[1] According to the book of Philemon, he was in prison with Paul when Colossians was written.

While in prison, Epaphras was "wrestling in prayer" for his brothers and sisters back home. We can surmise that he was tremendously concerned over the heresy that was circulating through the church. These people were his spiritual children, and he was burdened for them.

As discussed in the introduction of this book, it was heresy that prompted the epistle from Paul. The Colossians needed to understand who Christ really was and who they were in Him so that they might fend off the false teaching that was trying to infiltrate their thinking. Perhaps the same heresies were troubling the Laodiceans, since the letter was to be passed on to them.

Most of us have seen someone who was trained in Christian faith veer off into unbiblical doctrine. It is tragic, especially if you happened to be that person's pastor, Sunday school teacher, or mentor. Sons and daughters of some of the world's most famous evangelical teachers have abandoned basic biblical principles for self-designed religion or for another faith system. But sometimes we Christians spend a great deal of time nitpicking at each other over doctrinal issues that are not as critical as we imagine instead of equipping our children and new believers to identify heresy and steer clear. It is good to debate and discuss different doctrinal viewpoints. But it is a matter of grave importance for every believer to be educated in the non-negotiable points of doctrine, such as the deity of Christ. Even then, some will choose to go a different way. We pray for them. But we do not bear guilt for their choices.

LUKE AND DEMAS (COL. 4:14)

Further greetings come from Luke and Demas to the people of Colossae. This Luke is the same one who wrote one of the gospels and the book of Acts. He was a faithful companion to Paul, but Demas would not remain so faithful. Though serving with Paul at the time this epistle was written, he would later desert Paul "because he loved this world" (2 Tim. 4:10). Again, the servant of the Lord who brings others to Christ and labors to disciple them is not responsible if they fall away. We can invest only so much despair into these losses; they will happen. As we see, even the great apostle Paul experienced these disappointments with people in whom he'd invested.

It is clear that the brothers and sisters in Colossae were in some sort of relationship with the church members in Laodicea. Paul, as evangelist to the nations, had a big-picture view of the church. He did not hesitate to ask one congregation to help another financially or to pass on letters. If there was no "Jew" nor "Greek" in Christ, then connections between congregations made sense.

Most certainly the same is true today. In north Seattle, where my husband and I minister, many of the churches make an effort to live as a greater Christian community. We have sunrise services together at Easter and an annual joint worship service in the summer. The youth pastors meet together, and the senior pastors meet together. Members of the Foursquare church near us volunteer at our foodbank; we refer people to each other for particular needs, and so on. The goal of our united group is that together we, the body of Christ, can meet the spiritual and physical needs of North Seattle. In isolation, we are far less effective.

NYMPHA (COL. 4:15)

Paul sends greetings to Nympha and the church in her house. There was no such thing as a church building until the mid-third century. Churches met in large homes, and sometimes they broke into smaller groups in a variety of homes, just like the "small groups," "cells," or "home groups" a church may have today. Scholars think that because Nympha had a home large enough to house a church, she may have been a wealthy widow. We can find nothing in the Scripture, however, to indicate that she wasn't married at the time. It has often been assumed she was unmarried because no husband is mentioned in connection to her. Such an assumption is unfounded, and it is concerning, in that it implies that if a man were around he is the one who would be mentioned, not Nympha.

Whatever the case, we see here one of many instances of a woman playing an important role in the early church. LaCelle-Peterson writes:

> The cultural blinders of recent centuries led generations of historians to assume that only men were leaders, partly because the church has so assiduously ignored the activities of actual women and looked only to the texts that restricted their involvement. . . . Women held leadership roles in at least some New Testament churches. . . . Paul commended many women for their efforts as missionaries, as servants of the church (a term he also used to refer to himself and Timothy and other prominent male leaders), as "those who worked hard for the gospel," and even as an apostle (Junia). . . . Paul expected women to pray and prophesy in public worship, hence his long discussion in 1 Corinthians 11:3–16 on how they should appear when they do so.[2]

I don't know whether Nympha was the leader of her home church or the host. No one can say for sure. But I do know that the roles described above are more comprehensive than teaching the children's Sunday school class or preparing the potluck, which have traditionally been regarded as places of service for women in the church. I'm not saying that those ministries aren't important. I am saying that women are not limited to these roles when it comes to leadership within the church.

REFLECTION QUESTIONS

1. Have you ever wrestled in prayer over someone else's struggles?

2. Why shouldn't a teacher or leader be held responsible for the backsliding of someone they've trained? What *is* the teacher responsible for?

3. What is your response to the quote from LaCelle-Peterson?

4. What role has God asked you to play in helping to spread the gospel and move the church forward?

29

A MODEL OF USEFULNESS

COLOSSIANS 4:16–17

In the quirky movie *Napoleon Dynamite*, Napoleon's friend Pedro is running for class president. Both of the boys are hopelessly socially awkward, it would seem, and Pedro has no chance of even being taken seriously. But at the school assembly where the candidates give their campaign speeches, Napoleon does something completely unexpected. After Pedro's disastrous speech, Napoleon hands a cassette to the sound man then gets on stage and dances. His dance is phenomenal. The student body goes wild, and Pedro winds up winning the election. It's a fun demonstration of a friend putting his fear and inhibition aside, selflessly offering up a hidden skill to aid a friend. If Paul had any reservations about using his gifts to educate the Christians of the world, he suppressed them for the cause of the gospel.

THE TWO LETTERS (COL. 4:16)

Two letters, which are to be traded, are mentioned in this verse: the present epistle, and a letter Paul wrote to the Laodiceans. It is not known what happened to the Laodicean letter. One theory is that it is actually the book of Ephesians. Though that book is addressed to the Ephesians, it doesn't list particular names, so the general address to the Ephesians could have been added later by someone other than Paul.

We did discover in a previous study that Onesimus and Tychicus were probably carrying both the letters of Colossians and Philemon to the Lycus Valley. The letter we know as Ephesians might have been part of that delivery bundle. But these ideas are just theories. Thousands of years later, we people of the Lord trust that the material God wanted in the New Testament survived and made it in. That's what matters.

A WILLINGNESS TO BE USED (COL. 4:16)

Paul recognized when he was being used of the Lord. He did not consider it boastful to tell others to look to his life as an example (see 1 Cor. 11:1). Nor did he think it was unseemly to expect others to receive his letters as

God-inspired missives or to pass them around to fellow congregations.

Paul's focus was on making the principles of Christianity clear to the people of his day. It likely never occurred to him that his letters would be read by believers over two thousand years in the future! But without his writings, you and I would be in the dark about many things. The letters of Paul contain some of the greatest exposition of our essential doctrine and are cherished by Christians everywhere.

Imagine if Paul had said, "I can't be used of God. Before I met Jesus, I persecuted Christians! How could God possibly use a sinner like me?" If he thought that way, he might never have gone on his foreign missions, which changed the world. Nor would he have written his authoritative letters, which continue to change people. Paul was bold for Christ because when he gave himself to Him, he completely shed his old self and embraced the "new man." He did not have to answer to anyone for what he had once been, and he expected that people would readily look to him as a model for the man he was now, without bringing up his past. Was he brazen to do so? Not at all. He was doing *exactly what God wanted him to do*: "forgetting what is behind and straining toward what is ahead" (Phil. 3:13).

Unfortunately, not all Christians gobble up grace as completely as Paul did. Some convince themselves that because they have made mistakes in the past, they aren't usable in the present. This is like sampling grace rather than making a full meal of it. Christ forgives who we were before we knew Him, and He forgives sins and mistakes that we've made since we've come to know Him. Our only correct response is to slough off our sin and our insecurities and stand at the ready for God's use.

Some Christians don't have a lot in their pasts to concern them, but they hesitate to be used by God because they are crippled by a general feeling of inadequacy. With a world out there that needs saving, it is almost self-indulgent to let oneself be hampered by low self-esteem. The fact is that God has given each of us gifts and abilities and He expects— He *needs*—us to use them.

And sadly, others of us downplay our usefulness as a sneaky way to garner a little praise. Sometimes I wonder whether God rolls His eyes when people coyly say, "Oh, no, I'm not good enough. . . . You should get someone else." Why not get about the business of the Lord, owning up to the fact that you've been equipped by Him with gifts He intends to use? Basking in false humility is a waste of time and hampers the work of the kingdom.

Denying one's talents and gifts is not humility. Humility is acknowledging that your abilities are from God, not yourself, and using those abilities to His glory, not your own. Humility is understanding that there is a kingdom purpose for your talents and making sure they are used for that. Paul knew that his letters were inspired by God and were necessary for firmly establishing the faith around the world, and he made that happen. He used his gifts for the kingdom and didn't stall things by being shy about it.

Finally, some are too selfish or lazy to use their gifts for the kingdom. Paul could have reasoned: "I should probably write a letter to the Colossians. They've got problems. But hey! Their problems aren't as bad as mine! I'm in jail, for crying out loud. They should be sending *me* letters!" It is easy to justify doing nothing. No one had better excuses than Paul—yet his ministry never stopped. He remains a role model to this day. He persevered in ministry through times of great struggle; we set our ministry aside to watch football. The Lord can find others to do His work, but what a loss to the person who deprives herself of the chance to serve Him!

ARCHIPPUS (COL. 4:17)

We do not know what ministry Archippus, who was a member of Philemon's household (see Philem. 2), was to complete. We do not know why he needed encouragement. Was the task arduous, and he had grown weary? Or was he lazy and neglectful? We do not have enough details to draw conclusions. As seen above, however, if anyone had the right to call a person back to steady service for the Lord, it was Paul.

In October 2018, Alex Honnold became the first person to climb El Capitan in Yosemite National Park without any ropes.[1] He scaled that massive rock with just his hands and feet. It was a shocking accomplishment that took untold tenacity. The whole country lauded him for what he did. The things that God asks us to do for the kingdom may never attract much attention. We may think our deeds are unimpressive—nothing like the feat Honnold pulled off. But consider this: our efforts, which may seem meager to us, will be used of God in the lives of other people. They will move the eternal kingdom of God forward. That is no small thing, now, is it? Inviting a homeless person to eat with you, teaching a child to pray, preaching a well-prepared sermon, passing out cups of cold water to protestors at a rally for something you may not even support—surely these selfless acts are, in the end, more monumental than scaling an enormous rock mountain.

To serve the Lord in any ministry capacity is an honor. Whenever we are entrusted to do so, we should rejoice and work with diligence. A glance through the book of Colossians will remind us what God has done for us. What a privilege to respond by being of use to His kingdom!

REFLECTION QUESTIONS

1. What gifts do you have that are useful for the kingdom? How are you employing them, or how should you be?

2. Do you have a tendency toward laziness? Or is there any desire for you to use your gifts and talents to glorify yourself?

3. Perhaps you are a faithful servant who is starting to grow weary. If so, what is causing your weariness? Call upon the Holy Spirit to reveal what you must do so your passion can be reignited.

4. Take a moment and rededicate your time and talents to the Lord's work. Listen carefully; He may reveal to you something new that He wants you to do.

30

PAUL: HIS VULNERABILITY AND HIS BENEDICTION

COLOSSIANS 4:18

A couple of decades ago my purse was stolen. Back then it was fairly common to carry a checkbook. I had one, and I had credit cards in my wallet as well. The thief ran off with all of it. I thought she would use my credit cards, but I was wrong. She only used my checks. She signed my name to them when she purchased items totaling nearly two thousand dollars. The cashiers accepted the checks without asking for a driver's license to look at my picture and verify whether or not this woman was me.

Eventually my bank returned those checks to me. It was jarring to see someone sign my name with a style of handwriting that wasn't even remotely close to mine. Why didn't the woman use my credit cards? Perhaps it was because at that time, cashiers were trained to be diligent about comparing the signature on a sales slip to the signature on the back of the credit card. A signature is very personal and distinctive thing. Unless the purse snatcher had been a trained forger, the difference between her writing and mine would have been spotted immediately.

PAUL'S OWN HAND

Even in our technological age, a signature is often required to prove the origin of a document. Sometimes an "electronic signature" done with a computer is enough, but other times we are required to use an actual pen and physically sign something. From Paul's time to ours, handwritten signatures have been valued because they are distinctive.

Paul understood the power of handwriting his own name. After dictating the contents of his letter, he personally gave his own signature to it. Since he mentions that fact, we know it was important to him that the readers were aware of it. He may have done so to assure its authenticity to the Colossians. It could have been catastrophic to the Colossians' understanding of Christianity (and maybe even ours!) if someone with ill intent—or even just with limited knowledge and wisdom—had written the letter and claimed it was from Paul. New Christians were aware that Paul was a true apostle from God, so it would have been an important assurance to know that the letter they received really did come from him.

Apparently his signature and his written verification of its authenticity provided adequate proof for the recipients. The other reason for signing a letter is to give it a personal touch. Have you ever received a printed letter with an electronic signature that is made to look like it has been written in ink? Once you realized it wasn't actually handwritten, didn't you feel a little less connected to the sender? Knowing someone spent a moment actually signing something indicates that they thought of you and that the message is from them to you, not from a machine to you. Signing by hand communicates that the letter is heartfelt.

Additionally, signing his name could have been difficult for Paul. He was getting older, and perhaps his imprisonment involved physical limitations. Also, experts widely theorize that Paul had poor eyesight, which is why he would have had someone else write the rest of the letter under his dictation. Placing his name by his own hand at the end of the letter wasn't just an authenticating seal. It was a symbol of his affection.

PAUL'S CHAINS

Though in prison, Paul's mind was sharp, and he was certainly full of the Holy Spirit. He served the Lord through the writing of his epistles. He never came close to complaining. Quite the opposite! He was full of thanksgiving and praise.

He allowed himself one simple plea at the end of his brilliant, instructive, enriching letter: "Remember my chains." *Don't forget I'm still in prison.* Between the Colossians and Paul, Paul was the authoritative one. But he needed something from them. He needed their prayers. This plaintive request is a reminder of the equality that Paul taught in the previous chapters. Though he functioned as a leader and role model to them, he was not above them.

We should never expect our spiritual leaders to be perfect human beings. But nor should we expect that their lives are smoother sailing than anyone else's. A spiritual leader's job is to shoulder a heavy load, ministering to her people whenever they need her, especially if she is in paid full-time ministry. But scripturally speaking, it is also God's expectation of every believer that they serve and love and care for every other believer—even the paid ones.

The fact that someone is in full-time ministry doesn't mean he doesn't grow weary, have family problems, or worry about money. We expect our spiritual leaders to show considerable concern for our needs, and that is as it should be. But we must also remember that sometimes their personal problems are looming in the background. Should they stop caring for their people? No, of course not. But we could remember their needs as well and respond with prayers and practical expressions of love.

PAUL'S BENEDICTION

As mentioned in our very first study, Paul couldn't actually impart God's grace on anyone. Only Jesus could do that. But one of the ways in which Christians have always shown love for each other is to speak God's blessing over one another in this fashion. The grace of God was already part of the Colossians' lives; Paul wasn't giving it to them. Rather, it was Paul's hope that they would be keenly aware of it. That they would feel it. Perhaps when we speak grace over others we are really praying that God will send some small reminder their way that they are already the recipients of His grace.

Words concerning grace are all over the pages of Colossians. We read that grace has delivered us from the dominion of darkness (1:13). Grace ended our alienation from God (1:21) and reconciled us to Him (1:22). Through grace the great mystery dwells within us (1:27). It is grace that brought us from death to life and canceled our legal indebtedness (2:13–14). Grace set us free from human regulation (2:16, 17). Because of grace, we will appear with Christ in glory (3:4). Indeed, we have many reasons to be thankful, and we have spent many pages in this study book in exploration of God's grace in us. To remind one another of this and to speak benedictions of grace is a holy and love-filled act.

And so, reader and sibling in Christ, permit me to speak it over you: *Grace be with you.*

REFLECTION QUESTIONS

1. Why do you think it was important for Paul to personally sign the letter he was sending?

2. Is there someone in ministry who could use encouragement from you this week? What could you do for that person?

3. What have you learned about God's grace from Colossians?

NOTES

INTRODUCTION

1. N. T. Wright, *Colossians and Philemon* of Tyndale New Testament Commentaries, vol. 12, ed. Leon Morris (Downers Grove, IL: InterVarsity Press, 1986), 37.

2. See F. F. Bruce, *The Epistles to the Colossians, to Philemon, and to the Ephesians*, The New International Commentary on the New Testament (Grand Rapids, MI: Wm. B. Eerdmans Publishing Company, 1984), 5.

3. A significant voice of disagreement is Morna D. Hooker. "The strangest feature about this reconstruction of the situation behind the Colossian epistle is the extraordinary calm with which Paul confronts it. If there were within the Colossian Christian community any kind of false teaching which questioned the uniqueness of Christ . . . Paul would surely have attacked such teaching openly and explicitly." *From Adam to Christ: Essays on Paul* (Eugene, OR: Wipf and Stock Publishers, 1990), 122.

4. N. T. Wright, *Colossians and Philemon*, 25.

5. See F. F. Bruce, *The Epistles to the Colossians, to Philemon, and to the Ephesians*, The New International Commentary on the New

Testament (Grand Rapids, MI: Wm. B. Eerdmans Publishing Company, 1984), 22.

6. Arthur G. Patzia, *Ephesians, Colossians, Philemon*, Understanding the Bible Commentary Series (Grand Rapids, MI: Baker Books, 2011), 5.

7. Patzia, *Ephesians, Colossians, Philemon*, 5–6.

8. Patzia, *Ephesians, Colossians, Philemon*, 6–7.

DEVOTION 1

1. Larry Stone, "Inside the Room: Edgar Martinez Brings His Trademark Cool to Hall of Fame Moment," *The Seattle Times*, January 22, 2019, www.seattletimes.com/sports/mariners/edgar-martinez-brings-his-trademark-cool-to-hall-of-fame-moment/, accessed February 2019.

2. While NIV uses the term *holy people*, the NRSV uses the word *saints*.

DEVOTION 3

1. A discussion of the possible heresies is found in the introduction under "The Reason."

2. Bruce B. Barton, Mark Fackler, Linda K. Taylor, and Dave Veerman, *Philippians, Colossians, Philemon*, Life Application Bible Commentary, edited by Philip Comfort (Wheaton, IL: Tyndale House Publishers, Inc., 1995), 154. The NIV reads "all the wisdom and understanding that the Spirit gives." Other translations read "all spiritual wisdom and understanding." To the second translation, Ralph Martin said: "[These two words are] qualified by the adjective 'spiritual,' which is not a courtesy reference but a direct appeal to the Holy Spirit whose help is invoked to make it a valid prayer request." Ralph Martin, *Ephesians, Colossians, and Philemon: Interpretation: A Bible Commentary for Teaching and Preaching* (Louisville, KY: Westminster John Knox Press, 1991), 103.

3. See F. F. Bruce, *The Epistles to the Colossians, to Philemon, and to the Ephesians*, The New International Commentary on the New Testament (Grand Rapids, MI: Wm. B. Eerdmans Publishing Company, 1984), 50.

4. Barton et al., *Philippians, Colossians, Philemon*, 158.

DEVOTION 4

1. Scholar Morna Hooker argues that no evidence exists of any such hymn. *From Adam to Christ: Essays on Paul* (Eugene, OR: Wipf and Stock Publishers, 1990), 122.

2. Arthur G. Patzia, *Ephesians, Colossians, Philemon*, Understanding the Bible Commentary Series (Grand Rapids, MI: Baker Books, 2011), 29–30.

3. Patzia, *Ephesians, Colossians, Philemon*, 24.

4. According to F. F. Bruce and others, Paul understood the pre-existent Christ as the personification of Wisdom, and Wisdom was known as the "master workman" (i.e., Creator). See F. F. Bruce, *The Epistles to the Colossians, to Philemon, and to the Ephesians*, The New International Commentary on the New Testament (Grand Rapids, MI: Wm. B. Eerdmans Publishing Company, 1984), 62.

5. Patzia, *Ephesians, Colossians, Philemon*, 30.

6. Bruce B. Barton, Mark Fackler, Linda K. Taylor, and Dave Veerman, *Philippians, Colossians, Philemon*, Life Application Bible Commentary, edited by Philip Comfort (Wheaton, IL: Tyndale House Publishers, Inc., 1995), 164.

7. The Salvation Army International, *The Salvation Army Handbook of Doctrine* (London: Salvation Books, 2010), xv. Doctrine 2 states: "We believe that there is only one God, who is infinitely perfect, the Creator, Preserver, and Governor of all things, and who is the only proper object of religious worship."

8. N. T. Wright, *Colossians and Philemon* of Tyndale New Testament Commentaries, vol. 12, ed. Leon Morris (Downers Grove, IL: InterVarsity Press, 1986), 78.

9. The Greek in this passage is unclear. Either God was pleased to have His fullness dwell in Christ, or Christ was pleased to have the fullness of God dwell in Him, or the fullness of God (as the subject) was pleased to dwell within Christ. In any case, the point is that the fullness of God did dwell in Jesus Christ.

DEVOTION 5

1. We might argue here that even good deeds motivated by a burdened conscience are selfish because they are done to soothe the conscience. But if we follow that argument too far, we find ourselves questioning the motive of every deed of every human, saved or unsaved. Even acts done as a response to the prompting of the Holy Spirit could come under suspicion. At some point, it is fair to say that through the grace God has placed in our lives, humans are capable of doing a truly righteous thing. Prevenient grace says that this is possible even before salvation.

2. Elisha Albright Hoffman, "Glory to His Name," in *The Songbook of The Salvation Army*, North American Edition (Alexandria, VA: The Salvation Army, 2016), #76.

3. Stuart Townend, "How Deep the Father's Love for Us," in *The Songbook of The Salvation Army*, North American Edition (Alexandria, VA: The Salvation Army, 2016), #32.

4. John Wesley talked about "Christian perfection" because he did not consider ungodliness that was out of ignorance, as opposed to intention, to be sinful. The Christian was "perfect" in that every known part of him/herself in thought, word, and deed was fully submitted to God.

5. N. T. Wright, *Colossians and Philemon* of Tyndale New Testament Commentaries, vol. 12, ed. Leon Morris (Downers Grove, IL: InterVarsity Press, 1986), 87.

6. John Bakewell, "Hail, Thou Once Despisèd Jesus," in *The Songbook of The Salvation Army*, North American Edition (Alexandria, VA: The Salvation Army, 2016), #167.

DEVOTION 6

1. Arthur G. Patzia, *Ephesians, Colossians, Philemon*, Understanding the Bible Commentary Series (Grand Rapids, MI: Baker Books, 2011), 40.

2. Patzia, *Ephesians, Colossians, Philemon*, 40–41.

3. Patzia, *Ephesians, Colossians, Philemon*, 41.

4. F. F. Bruce, *The Epistles to the Colossians, to Philemon, and to the Ephesians*, The New International Commentary on the New Testament (Grand Rapids, MI: Wm. B. Eerdmans Publishing Company, 1984), 85.

5. N. T. Wright, *Colossians and Philemon* of Tyndale New Testament Commentaries, vol. 12, ed. Leon Morris (Downers Grove, IL: InterVarsity Press, 1986), 96.

DEVOTION 7

1. John Gowans, "They Shall Come from the East," in *The Songbook of The Salvation Army*, North American Edition (Alexandria, VA: The Salvation Army, 2016), #1011.

2. Brenda Salter McNeil, *A Credible Witness: Reflections on Power, Evangelism, and Race* (Downers Grove, IL: InterVarsity Press, 2008), 16.

3. Arthur G. Patzia, *Ephesians, Colossians, Philemon*, Understanding the Bible Commentary Series (Grand Rapids, MI: Baker Books, 2011), 47.

4. Modern English Version translation from the Greek refer to orderliness and stability/steadfastness. The NIV translation is different and doesn't seem to have as much support.

DEVOTION 8

1. N. T. Wright, *Colossians and Philemon* of Tyndale New Testament Commentaries, vol. 12, ed. Leon Morris (Downers Grove, IL: InterVarsity Press, 1986), 105.

2. Frederick William Danker, editor, *A Greek-English Lexicon of the New Testament and other Early Christian Literature — Third Edition* (Chicago, IL: The University of Chicago Press, 2000), 955.

DEVOTION 9

1. C. S. Lewis, *Mere Christianity* (New York: Touchstone, 1952), 56.

2. The Salvation Army International, *The Salvation Army Handbook of Doctrine* (London: Salvation Books, 2010), xv. Doctrine 3 states: "We believe that there are three persons in the Godhead — the Father, the Son and the Holy Ghost, undivided in essence and co-equal in power and glory."

DEVOTION 10

1. F. F. Bruce, *The Epistles to the Colossians, to Philemon, and to the Ephesians*, The New International Commentary on the New Testament (Grand Rapids, MI: Wm. B. Eerdmans Publishing Company, 1984), 103–104.

DEVOTION 11

1. F. F. Bruce, *The Epistles to the Colossians, to Philemon, and to the Ephesians*, The New International Commentary on the New Testament (Grand Rapids, MI: Wm. B. Eerdmans Publishing Company, 1984), 108–109.

2. Martin Luther, quoted in Donald G. Bloesch, *Christian Foundations: Jesus Christ, Savior & Lord* (Downers Grove, IL: InterVarsity Press, 1997), 144.

3. Hendrikus Berkhof, *Christian Faith: An Introduction to the Study of the Faith* (Grand Rapids, MI: Wm. B. Eerdmans, 1986), 306.

4. F. F. Bruce, *The Epistles to the Colossians, to Philemon, and to the Ephesians*, 110–111.

5. F. F. Bruce, *The Epistles to the Colossians, to Philemon, and to the Ephesians*, 111.

DEVOTION 12

1. F. F. Bruce, *The Epistles to the Colossians, to Philemon, and to the Ephesians*, The New International Commentary on the New Testament (Grand Rapids, MI: Wm. B. Eerdmans Publishing Company, 1984), 116.

2. Baptism is not officially celebrated in The Salvation Army to underscore this very point. We stress sacramental daily living over sacramental incidental practices. However, our refraining from water baptism is not a criticism of it.

3. In the interest of full disclosure, I must make mention that my family and I observe a twenty-four-hour Sabbath for rest and worship every Saturday evening through Sunday evening. We are able to do this even as pastors because we are fully prepared for Sunday by 6 p.m. Saturday night, and we regard Sunday morning preaching and teaching as worship, not labor. Just as Jesus allowed His disciples to pick corn on the Sabbath, we have found that there are some Sundays when we can't reasonably be too stringent. But we have found that our Sabbath practice has had tremendous spiritual, emotional, and physical benefit. Sabbath is mentioned in the Ten Commandments, and we still give sacred credence to the other nine in that list. In light of Colossians 2, which specifically mentions Sabbath when it eschews the mandate to observe holy days, I could never assert that Sabbath remains an obligatory practice. But I will always recommend it as a better way to live.

4. Plato, *The Republic*, Dover Thrift Edition, ed. Joslyn T. Pine (n.p.: Dover Publications, 2000), book VII.

5. N. T. Wright, *Colossians and Philemon* of Tyndale New Testament Commentaries, vol. 12, ed. Leon Morris (Downers Grove, IL: InterVarsity Press, 1986), 125.

6. C. S. Lewis, quoted in Art Lindsley, "C. S. Lewis on Humility and Pride," www.cslewisinstitute.org/C.S._Lewis_on_Humility_and_Pride, accessed February 2019.

7. The Salvation Army International, *The Salvation Army Handbook of Doctrine* (London: Salvation Books, 2010), xv. Doctrine 2 states: "We believe that there is only one God, who is infinitely perfect, the Creator, Preserver, and Governor of all things, and who is the only proper object of religious worship."

8. Louis Giglio, *The Air I Breathe: Worship as a Way of Life* (Colorado Springs, CO: Multnomah, 2017), 3.

DEVOTION 13

1. PursueGod Community, "The Rules of the Pharisees," www.pursuegod.org/rules-pharisees/, accessed February 2019.

2. In The Salvation Army, a soldier agrees to live by certain standards. They may seem like a list of rules—soldiers don't drink or smoke, soldiers contribute financially to the ministry, etc.—but these standards are not superimposed on all Christians as a matrix by which to evaluate their sincerity.

DEVOTION 14

1. The Salvation Army International, *The Salvation Army Handbook of Doctrine* (London: Salvation Books, 2010), xv. Doctrine 3 states: "We believe that there are three persons in the Godhead—the Father, the Son and the Holy Ghost, undivided in essence and co-equal in power and glory."

2. This is the way it works in the United States. It varies in other countries.

DEVOTION 15

1. Ralph Martin, *Ephesians, Colossians, and Philemon: Interpretation: A Bible Commentary for Teaching and Preaching* (Louisville, KY: Westminster John Knox Press, 1991), 122.

2. Martin, *Ephesians, Colossians, and Philemon*, 123.

DEVOTION 16

1. F. F. Bruce, *The Epistles to the Colossians, to Philemon, and to the Ephesians*, The New International Commentary on the New Testament (Grand Rapids, MI: Wm. B. Eerdmans Publishing Company, 1984), 146.

DEVOTION 17

1. It was an important tenet of the Hebrew faith to be welcoming to "the stranger"—someone who was not Jewish by birth but would attach him/herself to the Jewish nation. There is also mention in the Old Testament of outsiders who converted to Judaism. (Ruth is an example.)

2. Briefly, the doctrine of election teaches that God chooses who can come to Christ for salvation and who cannot.

3. F. F. Bruce, *The Epistles to the Colossians, to Philemon, and to the Ephesians*, The New International Commentary on the New Testament (Grand Rapids, MI: Wm. B. Eerdmans Publishing Company, 1984), 146.

DEVOTION 18

1. John Wesley, www.christianity.com/bible/commentary.php? com=wes&b=51&c=3, accessed February 2019.

DEVOTION 19

1. See devotion 17.

2. N. T. Wright, *Colossians and Philemon* of Tyndale New Testament Commentaries, vol. 12, ed. Leon Morris (Downers Grove, IL: InterVarsity Press, 1986), 148.

DEVOTION 21

1. Reference to Paul's motives in giving the household tables. J. R. Porter, *The Illustrated Guide to The Bible* (New York, NY: Chartwell Books, 2016), 248.

2. Kristina LaCelle-Peterson, *Liberating Tradition: Women's Identity and Vocation in Christian Perspective* (Grand Rapids, MI: Baker Academic, 2008), 106.

3. It is most likely that the Greek word used here means specifically children who are still being raised and living in their parents' household. This is not about adult children. (Quoted by Peter T. O'Brien, *Colossians–Philemon*, Word Biblical Commentary, vol. 44, ed. David A. Hubbard and Glenn W. Barker [Grand Rapids, MI: Zondervan, 2000], 224.)

DEVOTION 22

1. Ralph Martin, *Ephesians, Colossians, and Philemon: Interpretation: A Bible Commentary for Teaching and Preaching* (Louisville, KY: Westminster John Knox Press, 1991), 128–129.

2. Arthur G. Patzia, *Ephesians, Colossians, Philemon*, Understanding the Bible Commentary Series (Grand Rapids, MI: Baker Books, 2011), 91–92.

3. Patzia, *Ephesians, Colossians, Philemon*, 92.

4. Just as Paul doesn't condemn slavery, he doesn't condone it. Nothing that is or is not in this passage should be taken to mean that Paul was in favor of the institution of slavery.

5. It may seem that the harsher words in this passage are reserved for slaves. Ephesians 6:5–9 is an almost identical passage, but in that instance the harsher words are given to the masters.

DEVOTION 26

1. Vincent J. Donovan, *Christianity Rediscovered* (Maryknoll, NY: Orbis Books, 2005), 49.

DEVOTION 28

1. Arthur G. Patzia, *Ephesians, Colossians, Philemon*, Understanding the Bible Commentary Series (Grand Rapids, MI: Baker Books, 2011), 100.

2. Kristina LaCelle-Peterson, *Liberating Tradition: Women's Identity and Vocation in Christian Perspective* (Grand Rapids, MI: Baker Academic, 2008), 153.

DEVOTION 29

1. *National Geographic*, October 3, 2018, www.national geographic.com/adventure/features/athletes/alex-honnold/most-dangerous-free-solo-climb-yosemite-national-park-el-capitan/, accessed February 2019.

ADDITIONAL BOOKS IN SERIES

Amy Reardon, *Holiness Revealed: A Devotional Study in Hebrews* (Indianapolis, IN: Wesleyan Publishing House, 2015).

Allen Satterlee, *Joy Revealed: A Devotional Study in Philippians* (Indianapolis, IN: Wesleyan Publishing House, 2017).

Allen Satterlee, *The Kingdom Revealed: A Devotional Study on The Sermon on the Mount* (Indianapolis, IN: Wesleyan Publishing House, 2018).

These resources are available at www.wphstore.com.